PROLOGUE

The Fingal Heritage Project in compiling their excellent booklet on 'Working Life in Fingal 1936-1959', have filled an important gap in recent history. All those who worked on, and assisted with the project are to be complimented.

It has been rightly mentioned in the booklet that working life has changed in Fingal. In one sense Fingal is a microcosm of the changes that have taken place in our entire country. The interviewing techniques used by the members of the team were handled very sensitively and the sections were linked expertly.

The thoughts and memories of all those contributing are of great value for current and future generations. This booklet will provide insight and understanding between the generations and is enjoyable to read.

The booklet covers the period from 1936, the date of the establishment of Aer Lingus, Aer Rianta, Bord na Mona and other state enterprises; it was also the year of my birth. The communications revolution commenced during the time covered by the booklet. During this period working life changed radically, affected by increased mechanisation, improved communications, the growth of technology and the initial introduction of part-time work, contract work and home working.

It has been a privilege for me, an 'incomer' to Fingal of only twenty years residence to have been asked to write the prologue for such an important work. All the more so as my late uncle Jim, my father Denis and I have had the pleasure of representing members of the Federation of Rural Workers and the Workers Union of Ireland from 1943 to 1976, in the Fingal area.

Jim Larkin
March 1994

INTRODUCTION

This booklet addresses the theme of working life in Fingal between 1936 and 1959 and is essentially a recording of the oral history of the men and women who worked there, in this period. The fundamentally rural landscape of Fingal, the traditional name for the area of North County Dublin defined by the River Tolka in the south and the River Delvin in the north, was changing and developing as new technology was introduced and the area was becoming urbanised. In 1936 work had started on the building of Dublin Airport, which as it grew encroached on land which for centuries had been worked and cultivated as farm land. The very landscape of Fingal itself was changing. However in 1959, just as the airport was about to enter a new decade with a confident and assured role in the country's economy, the Hill of Howth tramline was closed down. Sadly, it was deemed uneconomic and old fashioned, with no place in Dublin's modern transport system. These two events, just twenty-three years apart, are indicative of how much working life changed in Fingal. For example this was the period that saw the introduction of electricity to rural Fingal which brought with it profound changes to working life and the widespread use of farm machinery which changed the way farms were worked.

We talked to farmers, blacksmiths, parlour maids, potato sorters, soldiers, civil servants and many others about their working lives and we hope that their recollections and anecdotes can give some sense of what their working lives and the changes they experienced were like. How did farmers view the first tractors? How did World War II affect the work of blacksmiths? How did the building of Dublin Airport change working life?

We believe that these questions are best answered by the men and women we interviewed who worked at these jobs, trades and crafts and are now recorded in this booklet.

4

WORKING LIFE
IN FINGAL
1936 - 1959

RECOLLECTIONS
FROM
NORTH COUNTY DUBLIN

COPYRIGHT THE FINGAL HERITAGE GROUP 1994

PUBLISHED BY THE FINGAL HERITAGE GROUP

ACKNOWLEDGMENTS

THE FINGAL HERITAGE PROJECT

Project Co-Ordinators: Claire Campbell, Pat Hawes, Rory Keane.

Editors: Rory Keane, Claire Campbell, Bernadine Brady

Layout and Design: Deirdre Kelly

Illustrations: Kim Jenkinson

Research Assistants: Fiona Blaney, Mairéad Bonass, Bernadine Brady, Andrew Byrne, Rachel Byrne, Mary Caffrey, Gemma Clarke, Jennifer Clarke, Mary Clare Considine, Claudine Devlin, Jill Flanagan, Kim Jenkinson, Garret Kearns, Deirdre Kelly, Dominic Kenny, Rita Kinsella, Deborah Lambkin, Phillip Lee, Olivia McCormack, Mairéad McLoughlin, Muriel Redmond, Siobhán Walsh, Christian Wilde, Darren Wilde.

Our sincere thanks goes to the following people who agreed to be interviewed and without whose help this publication would not have been possible:-

Miriam Arthurs
Canon Brady
Christy Brown
Jack Buckley
Rose Canning
Bill Casey
Charlie Cawley
Mary Cawley
Owen Clarke
Joe Curtis
May Devlin
Sheila Fitzsimmons
Wilf Fitzsimmons
Una Fox
Pat French
Liam Gilmartin
Jenny Graham
Jim Hall

Bill Hamilton
Nellie Hamilton
Jack Harford
Maurice Hartigan
Kitty Hayes
Kitty Hughes
Maura Kavanagh
Maureen Lawless
Mary Lowndes
Desmond Lowham
Larry McNally
Eleanor McAllister
Noel McAllister
Paddy McDonagh
James Magill
Patsy Magill
Bernadette Marks

Tom Moore
Willie O'Brien
Gerry O'Malley
Joe O'Rourke
Shane Redmond
Tom Redmond
Peggy Reid
Joe Thompson
Tony Shaw
Simon Snow
Mary Warren
Maureen Weir
Bridget Whelan
Patrick Whelan
Peter Wilde

Special thanks to Ms. Mary Carmody and Ms. Linda Doran C.R.A.S., Ms. Margaret Lovatt, Training Advisor, and the management and staff of the FÁS Training Centre Baldoyle, Bernadette Marks, Swords Historical Society, The Department of Folklore, University College Dublin, Mona Hearn, Barnie Walsh and to Cathie Floirat for all her help with the research and editing.

The Fingal Heritage Project is sponsored by the Fingal Heritage Group.

Our thanks is extended to Fingal County Council who have sponsored the publication of this booklet.

This publication is the product of a FÁS training project which was funded by the local community, the employment levy and EU structural funds.

THE AIRPORT AND THE TRAMLINE

We were a colony overall. No matter what the railway had against you they daren't try to sack you, because if they interfered with you, the residents of the Hill of Howth, they'd pull the offices down. The local people, they kept the trams running.

Tom Redmond, who was a tram driver on the Hill of Howth tramline.

Why wouldn't you love to be in the Airport? The best job in Ireland. No matter what part of the Airport you worked, it was supposed to be one of the 'A' jobs in Ireland.

Patrick Whelan, who was a labourer at Dublin Airport.

One of the most drastic and visible changes to the nature of working life in Fingal was the construction of a commercial airport at Collinstown. Not only did the use of the land upon which the airport was built fundamentally change, but the airport brought new work opportunities to Fingal. Sadly, in parallel to the rise of the airport was the decline and eventual closure of the Hill of Howth tramline as it was seen as old fashioned and uneconomic. The way the transport infrastructure changed in Fingal in this period illustrates the way in which working life was changing, as the advances in technology and mechanisation brought new pressures and opportunities to North County Dublin and the people who lived and worked there.

Dublin Airport was officially opened on January 19th 1940 with the first flight from the airport being made by Aer Lingus to Liverpool. However the progress of World War II meant that the new airport was not to become fully operational until the end of the war. From 1917 to 1922, Collinstown had been the site of a Royal Air Force Aerodrome and like the other RAF aerodromes at Baldonnel, Gormanstown and Tallaght, was designated as a training depot station. When the British left Ireland the aerodrome was passed over to the Irish government and given to the Irish Air Corp. However they made Baldonnel the site of their headquarters and Collinstown was to remain unused until its development as a civil airport. Aer Lingus had been formed in 1936 and the national company was launched with some magnificent hyperbole.

Her scattered sons look homewards, proudly conscious of the Motherland's achievements in many spheres - not least her position in international transportation. Now are the 'Wild Geese' linked more closely to Eire, not only in spirit but in fact.

Advertising Copy for the launch of Aer Lingus.

Initially Aer Lingus had flown out of Baldonnel but, given that it was a military aerodrome, it soon became apparent that in the long term, if Irish aviation was to develop, a dedicated civil airport was going to be needed. This allied to the climate created by the Economic War with Britain and widespread unemployment meant that the decision to build the airport was made and Collinstown was chosen as its site. The work on the airport brought much needed employment to Fingal and despite the fact that a modern airport was being built the methods used illustrated the problems Ireland was facing industrially.

> *There was over a thousand men working on the construction of the runways here in '37, '38, '39, which was a tremendous amount of employment at that time. Most of them came from Swords. When the runway was being built it was all picks and shovels, horses as well. It was a grass field originally, the aircraft landed on grass but they had to excavate it and compact it and by and large it was quite satisfactory for the aircraft of the time.*

Owen Clarke who has worked at Dublin Airport since 1955.

The men employed would have traditionally found work within the agricultural community as labourers and the numbers employed shows the lack of mechanisation in the construction industry. In contrast when work commenced on laying the concrete runways in 1946, nine years later, only a hundred men as opposed to a thousand were employed as by then construction work was a lot less labour-intensive due to automation. The new airport's terminal building, which was built at this time, took its inspiration not from the air but from maritime travel. Flying in the forties was associated with the same ocean-going glamour of the more affluent classes.

> *The building (the original terminal building) was designed by Desmond Fitzgerald, an elder brother of Garrett Fitzgerald. He was an architect in the Office of Public Works. It was often said he had an ocean liner in his mind and certainly when it was in full operation and if you were over across the airfield and with all the windows lit up, it certainly resembled a liner at sea.*

Owen Clarke

The official opening of Dublin Airport in 1940 was followed by its occupation by an army garrison and once again the airport at Collinstown was in the hands of the military. As well as the airport's role in Emergency defences, land was given over to grow wheat and graze sheep to help ease the food shortages the country was experiencing and once the war ended, the airport provided some employment for de-mobbed men, keeping on some of the Emergency men stationed there and recruiting others with relevant experience.

> *Up to the end of World War II there was relatively few people working here. There was sheep grazing out in the field and there might be one flight a day or something like that but after World War II then obviously when the runways, the construction of the runways started a lot of people came, but that was obviously only for the duration of the runways being built. But some of the men were kept on as labourers and then you see, during the Emergency as we called it here, there was a big army and they were being de-mobbed after the war was over so, quite a lot of military men came here, particularly military policemen and they joined the security force here.*
>
> **Owen Clarke**

The only regular service was to Liverpool, with one arrival and departure a day and, apart from the occasional unauthorised landing by foreign military planes it was not until the end of the war when international civil aviation resumed, that the airport returned to normal. Throughout the post-war years the volume of traffic at Dublin Airport increased and the airport expanded into the surrounding land. The airport's physical expansion into rural Fingal was facilitated by long term planning. This and the changes in the area around the airport were all part of the area's urbanisation, which was changing the nature of working life in Fingal.

> *Gradually the airport extended and extended. We were always under the umbrella of the Department of, originally Industry and Commerce and later Transport and Power. But they made long term plans, 20 years, 25 years in advance to acquire land for runways and for airport development. So what they used to do was to negotiate with the landowners and if they came to an agreement they would buy the land and if it wasn't needed for 10 years, 15 years, they would rent it back on a year by year basis to the owner.*
>
> **Owen Clarke**

The land that was being bought up was predominantly farming land and obviously there were cases where farmers were reluctant to give up land which had been worked by their families for years, but in these cases the land was subject to compulsory purchase order. The coming of the airport had made it inevitable that the very fabric of Fingal, the land and the way it was worked, had to change.

> *But in cases where the people wouldn't sell and the property was needed for airport development, there's a legal thing that you call a compulsory purchase order. It was enforced and an independent arbitrator would decide on a fair price and the landowner would have to sell whether he wanted to or not.*
>
> **Owen Clarke**

This expansion brought jobs and increased opportunities to Fingal and for some the change of land ownership brought a change of employer.

> *The house I lived in belonged to a farmer. You know the lovely big, big mansion that's in front of it there? That's the farmer's. I was there a herd. A herd means a man that looks after sheep. They bought the farm, and the house I was living in. And of course they wanted to get me out. I said 'I can't. I have a wife and two children,' I said 'I'd get out of the house if they gave me a job in the airport.' Now I wasn't a tradesman, I was only a labourer. But I was jack of all trades in it. I'd drive tractors, I drove a lorry, anything, I'd drive around the airport. I cut grass, I was with fitters, I was a carpenter's helper.*
>
> **Patrick Whelan**

Just as the airport was growing in size and volume of traffic, so the sense of community amongst those who worked there was developing.

> *Sport was another area, there was always footballers of course, and Aer Lingus started a social club. There was one playing field, a soccer pitch, here at the airport and they had a club-house rented in Berkeley Place near Gardiner Street. It was a nice place, I used to walk in from Drumcondra and you know they used to have record recitals and there was a snooker table and you played darts and you could have a cup of tea and a biscuit for three pence or something like that. It was a friendly, social way to spend an evening.*
>
> **Owen Clarke**

And similarly, the employees spiritual as well as physical needs were administered to.

There was no church obviously at Dublin Airport, there is now, since 1964. But at that time there was no evening mass on a Saturday or no evening mass on a Sunday so, the only opportunity staff had, and it was a special concession, anybody working on a Sunday morning was permitted to go to mass if they could be released. So a priest used to come up, generally from Swords and we used to get Capuchin priests over from Raheny. And there was this temporary altar hawked around the place and set up in a hangar. I was often at a congregation like that at mass, I was looking down the wing of an aircraft or something like that. And local people used to come to mass as well.

Owen Clarke

Dublin airport entered the 1960's with an assured role in the country's economy. In 1958 not only had a terminal been opened, but the number of passengers it served had passed the half million mark. The airport was to continue to grow and be an important source of employment.

Now in the mid-50's it was a time like now of severe recession and it was a prime time for emigration. I remember the time when I must have written to fifty companies. I got a few interviews, it was only Aer Lingus where I knew I got a job. Otherwise I probably would have emigrated as a lot of my contemporaries did at that time, went to England because there was a building boom at that time after the war. Aer Lingus was on a par with the banks, they were considered great employment.

Owen Clarke

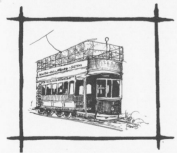 But in contrast to the growth and expansion of Dublin Airport at this time, the trams which since the late 19th century had served the community on the Hill of Howth were coming to the end of their service. In 1959 Coras Iompair Eireann (C.I.E.) closed down the Hill of Howth tramline, bringing to the end an institution which was much more than an impersonal facet of public transport but was a vital, integral part of the community on the Howth peninsula. Tom Redmond began his career as an electrician's helper with the Great Northern Railways (GNR) in Portadown before being transferred to Dublin to work in Connolly Station doing electrical maintenance work. After three years there he was moved to Sutton where after a year in maintenance, he was put on the trams as a driver, a job he had until 1959 when he drove the last tram before the line was closed.

I was transferred to Sutton. A man the name of Paddy Kelly was the maintenance man over the trams. I didn't know the first thing about trams. I didn't know the back from the front. I was there for twelve months to do the maintenance work on the trams and I was going into a depot which was a closed shop. The staffing that were employed from the beginning of the trams was handed down from father to son. I was a complete outsider, an intruder and I was working under very difficult conditions in comparison to the rest of the staff. I learned to become a tram driver. I took the tram out on the 20th March 1944. I got four hours tram driving and I was out as a tram driver.

Tom Redmond

In the 1930's Howth was served by three tram companies; the Dublin United Tramways Company Ltd. (DUTC), the Clontarf and Hill of Howth Tramway Ltd. (C&HHT) and the Great Northern Railways. The line of the DUTC was almost identical to that of the C&HHT, with both companies having agreed to inter-run over each other's track, but the line found it difficult to operate at a profit from the 1930's onwards. The closure of the C&HHT line in 1941 marked the beginning of the demise of trams as the main source of public transport in North County Dublin. The DUTC continued to operate, enjoying great rivalry with the tramline of the Great Northern Railways. However, in 1949 the DUTC was also forced to cease operations, leaving the GNR as sole custodian of the tram service.

The old Dublin United Tramway Company ran the trams from Nelson's Pillar to Howth. Now the situation was the GNR, they run the trains from Connolly Station of today, then Amiens Street, then to Howth, so one was run in opposition to the other. Now the old Dublin United saw where there was money to be made by opening up a tram line from Sutton Cross, to go right round the Hill of Howth and into the pier of Howth and the railway (GNR) saw where there was going to be more opposition. There was a competition between GNR and the old DUT Co. and the GNR won the day and they got the contract. They run trams round the Hill of Howth, to keep the old Dublin United from taking over the tram. Where the railway won was the people that would be using the trams would be serviced with a train service, where the Dublin United could only service them with a tram. The railway got the job.

Tom Redmond

Created in England by Bush Electric at the turn of the century, GNR trams were open-topped and, from the 1930's onwards had an attractive livery of cream and blue. Prior to the introduction of a central electrical system, trams were run on power generated locally.

The trams operated on its own fuse. It was run from Sutton, the Power House in Sutton. Then at the Hill of Howth, right at the summit, there was two houses there, and they used to change the batteries and when the ESB came along, that cut out the coal fire.

Tom Redmond

Conditions for the staff were often difficult. Hours were long with practically no breaks and the open topped design of the trams meant that the effects of the weather were always felt.

The trams ran in conjunction with the trains 6.20 am. until 11.20 pm. Then we were back in the depot at approximately 12.30 at night. Your working day was 12^1/$_2$ hours. No real break, you got no real break. Your wife or your son or your daughter would bring you what we called in those days a pint tommy can, with a can of tea and some sandwiches. The weather was the leading article. In the summer time it was perfect. In the winter time it was a nightmare because you were exposed to the weather. It was an open tram you see. You were standing on the front to drive, the rain was coming down your neck and you were washed off the tram. In summer time it wasn't so bad. It was more or less a bonanza in summer time.

Tom Redmond

Conditions were improved somewhat with the introduction of a union as the working day was shortened and the income was increased.

There was no union in the job and I forced a union into the job. I got them three raises while I was there. Your working day was reduced then to 8 hours.

Tom Redmond

There was more to working on the trams than just providing a transport service. Renowned for their kindness and courtesy, the tram drivers and conductors were known to provide an early wake-up call service and notify commuters of their arrival by ringing the tram's gong at their houses. They looked after children and elderly people and often allowed free travel to those unable to pay. Even the timetables of the trams were dictated by the needs of the community.

The first tram of the morning left the depot at 6.20 in the morning at Sutton. You went right round the hill which was 5½ miles approximately. On that run you bring the morning papers and you would deliver the morning papers to each house right around the Hill of Howth. Well in the winter time if we didn't see those people with light in the morning, knowing they were all passengers, when we'd be going round on our first trip to Howth, we'd knock on the door so as to have them ready to pick them up coming back. We done the church cars on a Sunday, for both churches, the Catholic and the Protestant. Different times to suit the churches. The first car on Sunday would be 7 am and you'd have one then for other denominations. It might be one o'clock the following morning before you'd be finished. That'd be into Monday. As long as the passengers were there, there was no question of time. Time didn't enter into it you just had to keep going. There was no regulation.

Tom Redmond

The service provided to the residents did not go unacknowledged. The kindness of the tram staff was reciprocated by the locals who showed their appreciation both financially and through their loyal support of the trams when they were in danger of extinction.

When Christmas would come, the fortnight before every Christmas, all the people were circularised with a circular not to forget the tram drivers and conductors. Three days before Christmas Mr. Campbell, who was a bank manager, would be in Sutton Station in the office. We were brought in, each member of the staff, driver and conductor got his Christmas present. That could be £100 and religiously ever year that was going to the drivers and conductors. You couldn't be sacked. No matter what the railway had against you, as far as credibility was concerned they daren't try to sack you because if they interfered with you the residents of the Hill of Howth, they'd pull the offices asunder, no one was ever sacked off the trams because it was the local people that kept the trams running.

Tom Redmond

But despite public contentment with the service, many factors were combining to force the closure of the tram system. The authorities of the GNR were anxious to stop running the trams, considering them uneconomical. The reason for their inefficiency was, it seems, partly due to bad control of finances as it was possible to buy a ticket which covered travel on both the train and tram at railway stations, but the GNR did not credit the trams with their share of the fare.

You could buy a combined rail and tram ticket at Connolly Station or any station that would bring you directly to the Hill of Howth, single or return. Now the tram was to get half of that money, but the tram never got the money. Although you were carrying a passenger, the tram was never in the benefit of carrying. We carried hundreds and thousands of people, but the tram wasn't credited with that. There's where the whole breakdown was, you know.

Tom Redmond

By 1947 the GNR was committed to the closure of the trams which they had allowed to fall into disrepair. The only factor preventing permanent closure was a statutory law which stated that if the trams were taken off they had to be replaced by an alternative service.

The authority of the depot in Sutton wanted to have the trams taken off. They let them fall into such bad repair. They didn't do any maintenance on them. They also let the tram tracks fall into decay and the trams would be coming, occasionally getting delayed.

Tom Redmond

The GNR had every reason to be concerned as the dominance which railways and trams had enjoyed in the realm of public transport for centuries was being eroded. Motor cars were becoming widespread and by the beginning of World War II, Dublin enjoyed a modern bus service. For the railways and trams, in spite of their poor state, the war provided temporary respite as petrol rationing made private motoring practically non-existent by 1942. After the war however car sales accelerated while the bus fleet continued to expand, servicing the new urban areas which were springing up all over Fingal. To survive, the GNR was forced to merge with CIE.

In 1958, CIE and GNR were both in a bad financial position. In other words, bus traffic and motor cars were putting public transport out of circulation. But they agreed, CIE and GNR agreed, that they would integrate with each other. It was agreed that CIE would take over the Republic end of the operation.

Tom Redmond

The end came quicker than was expected. In 1959, CIE suddenly stopped running the trams in spite of having assured the public that this would not happen. The tram service was to be replaced by buses.

In May 1959 the trams were taken off the Hill of Howth. No alternative service, no notification, no severance money, no nothing. The good Transport Union, I term it good, but I mean the reverse, decided and agreed it with CIE that when the trams would terminate an 31st May 1959 that the drivers and conductors would be replaced on the Dublin City Bus services. I was instructed by the chief inspector to do the last tram from Howth to Sutton which I duly done. I had no choice. I was under orders you see and went to Howth with my conductor. Colm Weafer was my conductor. We done the last tram from Howth.

Tom Redmond

The closure of the trams saddened many people who had treasured their value in non-monetary terms, not least of all the tram drivers and conductors who, after a lifetime of service on the trams, were forced to embark upon a new career.

Now I lost my job as a driver on a Saturday night, 31st May 1959. I was told to report on Monday morning to be a bus conductor at 47 years of age. We had an alterative, either go or be sacked. I with some of the other drivers were made conductors on the Dublin City Bus services as a spare and temporary man after all those years.

Tom Redmond

FARMING IN FINGAL

Working life in Fingal in the 1930's was still dominated by farming. For centuries the area's rich, fertile land had been cultivated and worked, and just as the land was shaped by agriculture, so the local economy was dictated to by the needs of rural communities. It was the modernisation and urbanisation experienced by people in North County Dublin which was to change a traditional pattern of working life that had its roots in the previous century. If there is one single event which serves as a paradigm for the changes people experienced in this period it is the gradual introduction of tractors onto farms, replacing the traditional power source, the horse. The ramifications of the mechanisation of farming were felt throughout the working community. Where possible, old crafts were adapted to meet new requirements; the drop in demand for labour as farming became less labour-intensive meant that agricultural labourers often faced either trying to get work in the county's nascent industries or emigration. Even the very shape of the lands changed as gates were widened and field size increased as economic necessity demanded that a greater return be made from the time and money invested in the land. Change was inevitable in Fingal, as it was in the whole of Ireland, and what is startling is how in less than a lifetime the way people worked and the jobs they had changed so radically. At the heart of the communities we looked at was the farm and a working life which was defined not in the urban measures of nine to five and Monday to Friday, but as a job which was the fulfillment of a lineal tradition. Farming then was not just a job, it was a way of life which demanded complete dedication to the land.

Farmers became landowners through inheritance, the land traditionally going to the eldest son and it was common for the younger members of the family to have to find work locally in urban areas or to emigrate. The average marriage age was late by today's standards and the farm was often handed over when the inheritor was getting married, as in the case of Noel McAllister a farmer from Donabate.

> *The uncle was a farmer. He had no children and I went in and started working the farm for him, you know and then inherited it. Very few people would acquire a farm any other way. Any of the farmers in the area, they're a dying breed here, they would have inherited through family inheritance. Very few of them would have had any money to buy a farm, I got the farm off him as a wedding present. It was the only way to do it to avoid death duty at the same time. The death duty was a killer.*

Noel McAllister

Figures had revealed that the average age at which women married in Ireland, 29 years, was the latest in the world. The men's average age of marriage was 35. Inability to marry earlier was put down to economic problems.

The Irish Independent, 13 May 1938

This situation often meant that fathers and grown sons worked together for years until the son could inherit the land and it was they, following traditional orthodoxy, who decided the way in which farms were run and not government policy or the recommendations of agricultural scientists. Farming was mixed in Fingal in this period, with the emphasis on maintaining a way of life.

It was more a way of life than a business. They never looked upon it as a business anyway. It was a way of life. As long as they made ends meet at the end of the day and they didn't owe any money. It was a very mixed farm, it was a bit of everything. Cattle, you had a few beef, the cows calved, he (Noel's uncle) milked them and he had a bit of milk for the house. He reared calves and he had a bit of grain, he'd have so many acres of barley and he'd sow his barley and wheat for feeding the cattle. It was a very small living he got out of it at that time.

Noel McAllister

You might call us tillage farmers. Mixed farming but mostly tillage. And just enough of dairy. A few cows for yourself and the few calves.

Maureen Lawless, who farmed in Swords.

Working the farm itself was hard physical labour and there was always work to be done not only tending crops and looking after livestock, but maintaining the fabric of the farm. The type of work that needed to be carried out would depend on the season and because the farms were mixed and oriented towards sufficiency there was always something to be done. Regardless of the time of year each day would start and end with milking and feeding the cows.

Well you'd get up in the morning at 7.30 and you'd milk the few cows, feed the calves. In the winter time you always had stall fed cattle and they were fed on pulp turnips, chopped up turnips. Ordinary turnips, they were grown for feed they were, mangles as well. They were all pulped up and crushed up and mixed in with oats and barley. But you always got up on Sunday morning to milk the cows and if you went to a match on Sunday afternoon you had to be sure you were back to milk the cows that evening.

Noel McAllister

Once the cows had been milked they would be taken out to pasture.

In the Autumn time you might buy in a few beasts, a few cattle, yearlings or something, and they'd come as wild as March hares, they wouldn't let you near them and you had some job trying to handle them. Ah, it was all physical work then. During the winter times when you fed the cattle, when you milked the cattle in the morning, you let them out, normally to the paddock. You always had one field then, so they wouldn't poach too much ground. You always had to have early grazing, you always protected that piece of grazing for early grazing.

Noel McAllister

The rest of the day would then be spent either picking turnips and mangels, which were grown to feed the cattle in the autumn and winter or clearing and checking the ditches and drains on the farm.

Then during the day you either went up and you picked turnips and you brought them in. That would be one or two days a week and the rest of the days you were up and you were cutting and breasting hedges, cleaning ditches, shovelling. You got into a ditch with a slash hook and you went the length of the ditch with the slash hook. It used to be you always had a hedge, a thorn hedge up to a bank. You'd have a ditch, but over the years the thorns, the briars would grow across that. So what you had to do was go along the hedge, cut that, the briars away from the hedge, cut it on the bottom, cut it on the side and roll it out with a fork. Just roll it out with a fork. You went the length of the ditch and it could be you were standing in a ditch with rubber boots and you could be up to nearly within an inch of the top of the boots, standing in water. And if you got a wet foot, then that's your hard luck! You were there for the day with a wet foot, you suffered for it the rest of the day. Or, when you came down for your lunch, you'd change your stockings. But you only had one pair of boots that had no holes in them.

Noel McAllister

Once the briars had been cleared from the ditch, the ditch itself was cleaned out and the drains were checked.

And then you came back then with a shovel and you shovelled down to the hard bottom. You opened up the drains and made sure all the drains were working O.K.

Noel McAllister

As winter advanced, the time arrived to plough the land and sow the crops; corn, potatoes and turnips. The traditional method of ploughing had been with a horse-drawn plough.

In the spring we ploughed the ground, harrowed and rolled it, to get it ready for the grain crop and vegetables. Getting the ground ready to set potatoes was a slow procedure, you tilled the ground very well before, my father would make drills with a plough and horse to set potatoes in. The men and myself would get the carts and load them with manure, go out to the fields where the drills were, the horse would walk up the centre of the drill slowly and you would throw the manure with a fork into the middle of the drills, taking two drills each side of your cart. When that was done you would bat the manure with a fork to spread it along the centre of the drill and dropped the seed potatoes from a large box into the drill, then my father would cover in the potatoes using a plough and a horse pulling it.

Miriam Arthurs from Swords who was born and worked on a farm.

However since the summer of 1919 when the Cork plant of Henry Ford started production of the Fordson tractor, tractors had started to become a more prevalent sight on Irish farms, and throughout this period more and more farmers started using them.

Whatever bit of ploughing you did, you normally started probably January in the wintertime a couple of days maybe. There was a tractor here when I came with a one sod plough and it was just, no cabin, an ordinary engine, four wheels and a seat on it. Basically nothing else, no protection from the elements. And you had, I remember a one sod plough, which was a very modern thing at that stage. And back and forward with the ploughing and you'd spend a lot of time (ploughing). There was 75 acres on the farm at that time. There would be about 30 acres tilled and the rest would be between potatoes and maybe a couple of acres of turnips and mangels for feeding cattle.

Noel McAllister

I used to be terribly lonely in the Spring. It was lovely to see them starting the corn crops and going out to work and seeing them later on. There was something creative about it, you know. Getting ready for it the next year, I loved the land and I loved the way you'd see things growing.

Maureen Lawless

Once the corn was sown it was traditional for the farmer's wife to bless the corn, to ensure the crop's fertility and the promise of a good harvest.

> *You used to go out when the corn was being sown and bless it. With the holy water over it. I remember that bit of it all right. The farmer's wife's job was to do that. She was told when to do that. She blessed the corn when they were getting ready to sow it.*
>
> **Maureen Lawless**

The labour intensive nature of farm work meant that it was necessary to employ labourers and both local men and women were hired to work on farms. Up until the late 50's labour was abundant in Fingal and there was no shortage of tasks for the workers.

> *Milking the cows and cleaning them out. Let them out on the grass, then I might have to feed horses in the yard. I might have to take the tractor out. Do a bit of ploughing. I was all around. I was a labourer. A labourer does everything.*
>
> **Patrick Whelan who worked as a farm labourer.**

> *Swords, when we started the farm up there it was easy enough getting help. Early 50's and that because there was everybody looking (for work). You used a lot of help in farming, getting your potatoes and the picking of them and the planting of them and cabbage and the Christmas sprouts and all that sort of thing. Then came all these factories to Swords and the airport started in a big way. So it was very hard then for a while to get labour.*
>
> **Maureen Lawless**

> *We always had a couple of full-time men and at busy times such as hay making and harvest time, casual workers would be brought in to help.*
>
> **Miriam Arthurs**

Just as the industrialisation of Fingal absorbed the traditional rural work force, as machinery was gradually introduced, primitive though it may have been, it not only improved working conditions on farms but reduced the number of people needed. The introduction of machines was fundamental in changing the way farms were worked. The tractor, being one of the first pieces of machinery to appear was greeted with a variety of emotions; fear, suspicion, but mostly delight.

I remember when the tractor came in first. My father kept saying 'Oh the land will be destroyed. Ah, the land, they're going too deep down and they're destroying the land!' Oh gosh it was terrific and sure you didn't know half how to use it some of the time. It was a great novelty, it was quite a big change on the farm. Done away with the horses and the carts. The pony and trap too. That took us to school in the early days, pony and trap. The doing away with them was a big thing and the coming of machinery. The older generation got it harder to accept, but we were younger at the time. You were made to accept change.

Maureen Lawless

You had the Ford and the diesel tractor, T20 diesel and it made farming a lot easier, a very economical tractor and they were very handy around the farm. They weren't too big, you could do anything from building to mowing, a great tractor.

Simon Snow, a farmer from Nevinstown Swords.

The advent of the tractor on the rural horizon marked the start of a gradual, but nevertheless, profound change in working methods. Just as farmers had to adapt their traditional techniques, so they tried to adapt their existing machinery to suit the new tractors; a physical union of the old and the new which highlighted the problems faced by farming in this period as the introduction of new technology had to be reconciled with old working methods and traditions.

I can remember the tractor coming in here first, it was sometime in the 50's. They'd put the tractor in front of these (the binder). They converted the front hitch of them and put a tractor in front but you see the tractor was a lot more powerful than two horses. These machines weren't geared for it and you had to be very careful because these things used to break down. They used to break down so much that he bought another one. He had another two of these. It was stupid really. It would have been better to have sold the two of them and to have bought a combine.

Noel McAllister

These developments changed not only the lifestyle and economic status of farming families, but the shape of the land and the way it was used.

It did change the land, the shape of the whole place. I put a lot of drains in and levelled a lot of ditches. It was a lot bigger. Instead of a five acre field you'll have a 25 acre field or 30 acre, to suit the machinery, to suit the tractors, you know.

Noel McAllister

The horse was gradually done away with. You had to feed the horse. It took nearly two acres of ground to feed the horse, you had actually the extra few acres.

Simon Snow

Regardless of the season there were always jobs around the farm which given the demands of being self-reliant had to be done, whether it was tending the vegetable garden or bringing in wood for the winter.

Well a very small amount (of potatoes) for the house, and we'd sell a few, an acre or two. They were very self-sufficient basically, very much self-sufficient. They used to have their own milk, they often churned their own butter at home. They all had a garden, had a vegetable garden, they used to grow their own vegetables. You always had cabbage and cauliflowers, carrots. Cutting hedges, maybe a tree would fall down, in the winter time for timber for the fire and things like that on spare days, it was all done by hand.

Noel McAllister

Perhaps the busiest and most important season on the farm was at harvest time when the corn would be reaped and then threshed by the steam powered mills. Not only did the harvest provide winter feed for cattle but it was an important cash crop.

21

He (Noel McAllister's uncle) had a bit of grain, he'd have so many acres of barley and he'd sow his barley and wheat for feeding the cattle, he'd sell the rest. You know the grain, it went to paying the overheads of the farm. Paying the rates which were big in those times in comparison, the rest then he'd live off it you know.

Noel McAllister

Autumn was the time when you hoped for a good harvest, that was the make or break time with the weather also, once you got the stooks of wheat, barley and oats into pikes and ricks, you would look for the mill to thresh the sheaves of corn.

Miriam Arthurs

A Compulsory Tillage Order had been imposed on farmers with the intention of boosting Irish grain supplies during World War II. Farmers had to devote more of their land to arable farming and at first this policy met with resistance as farmers were asked to change their traditional practices. Eventually more and more farms gave land over to tillage and obviously this increased the work for the threshing mills.

Our self-sufficiency policy was not as advanced as he had hoped, said Mr. de Valera in the Seanad, if farmers wanted to co-operate with the government they should now set about increasing the acreage under wheat.

The Irish Independent 5th October, 1939

Compulsory Tillage you're talking 1943-44, people that had grazing farms were compelled to break a portion of their farms and put it into corn. That was so we would have grain. Some people would rent the land out to others for tillage purposes, lots of people bought land at that particular era, people got out of marketing (market gardening) when the Compulsory thing came in.

Simon Snow

The threshing, which was the process of separating the ears of grain from the straw, started once the corn had been brought in. Before the use of combine harvesters, the harvest was either done by hand or by binders drawn by horses or tractors. The binders cut the corn and bound it together.

It wasn't done with a combine then, it was done with a pike. They stripped it and then they drew it in when it was seasoned and put it in ricks or in a hay barn. The farmers did their own harvesting, they cut it all, reap it and bind it, some of them had old scythes, hand work you know. They drew in their corn and it would be in ricks.

Jack Harford, who owned and operated threshing mills.

A binder was a very fragile thing. It just gathered it up and put it into sheaves and threw it out but it was a thing that I don't know how many times they were breaking down. They were a very fragile thing. They came before combines.

Maureen Lawless

Once the corn had been brought in the steam driven threshing mill would come to each farm and the corn would be threshed. In Fingal it was Jack Harford who, like his father before him, owned the mills and operated them.

There was threshing mills before the turn of the century, but when they came in first they were powered with portable steam engines which was pulled around by horses you see. But when my father got into it, he had the more modern stuff, the big steam threshing engines and threshing mills and that. And he got his first threshing mill at the turn of the century. You know, I grew along with them. So my father died of course, I was just 18 at the time and I had to go off and drive one of these engines and eh, I loved the bloody old engines.

Jack Harford

In Fingal the threshing was done with the assistance of a gang of local men hired in to work with the mill, unlike much of the rest of the country where larger farms had their own labourers to do the work.

The millman himself, that'd be the man, Jack Harford would be the man looking after the fire, to keep the thing going. There might be a second fella to give him a hand, 'cause he might have to go away or whatever. And there was the fella with the chaff and the two fellas at the top. Two, four and then six. God, there could be nine or ten! Because there would be fellas where the corn would be coming with the sacks and they'd be lifting it on their backs. Big heavy weights, sacks of fourteen stone.

Maureen Lawless

Well there was more employment wanted here, the farms were smaller here, all of them you know and for that reason they had to employ men. I'll tell you what, we'd get a farmer with rich corn and he'd be making deals on how much each man would get, six shillings or seven shilling, they'd be bargaining for hours to get it. I introduced another fashion as well, none of this bargaining now. I paid them a rate, the rate ended up at around a shilling an hour. Take on so many good men, you might see thirty or forty men looking for fourteen jobs. Ah sure there was a lot of sadness about really. The Economic War years when de Valera fell out with the British government, that created terrible problems. The only social life was hunger. Men there, if they didn't get employment, you'd see the tears there in their eyes coming out if there was nothing at home in the house.

Jack Harford

Just as farmers relied upon a good harvest to give them financial security for the coming year, so did agricultural labourers especially in a time notable for its economic hardship.

The mills were always a great money spinner for lads who had no work, who were unemployed. And I remember as a kid, a fight going on outside the yard, outside at seven o'clock in the morning between a gang that came from Lusk and Swords and both of them claimed that they were going to work the mill. I was only a kid at the time and it was a vicious, a very vicious fight. Apparently this Lusk crowd had been working the mill prior to this and the crowd from Swords arrived. And this was seven o'clock in the morning, they had walked from Swords and walked from Lusk!

Noel McAllister

Similarly Jack's day would start early and the only day that was not worked was Sunday.

No, we never threshed on a Sunday, but I would go on a Sunday evening and light up the fire in the engine and bank it down for Monday morning or if I had any little repairs to do on the thresher, small jobs, I'd go and do that. The main thing was you had to be ready to thresh at half past seven in the morning, you had to do nine hours work for the farmer. We'd come in with a few men and a thresher and all and set up the thresher. We had a threshing mill and an engine and we used to have a machine that used to tie the straw in round bundles and then we got balers for baling it in square bales. You know there was a lot of balers ticking around from World War One time. It was a laborious job I'll tell you.

Jack Harford

The anxiety which preceded a harvest, given the vagaries of the weather, because of its economic importance was released in the general feeling of festivity once it arrived. The combination of the magic of the big steam engines and the relief of a good harvest made it a celebratory time that involved everybody in the work.

I don't know if anyone can conceive what the mill was like. There was always a great air of festivity because you know, not alone did the workmen go from farm to farm, but we as kids used to go from farm to farm and follow it. And the porter, the big things of porter, would come out. It was hard work, now the mill was kept going, it had to keep going from seven o'clock in the morning till dark in the evening.

Noel McAllister

He was great, Jack Harford. He was I think about ten years older than me and when he came to our yards at home and you'd be a child, you see I wouldn't go to school that day for skins! He'd love to show you, he'd be always keeping' the mill going, puttin' on the coal, keepin' the steam up. It was a wonderful operation really.

Maureen Lawless

The day's threshing would end with the main mill workers being fed in the farmer's home.

Harvesting was thirsty work and important work so the workers needed to be well catered for with food and drink. Again, the woman of the house got down to work. They'd have help, but it was always a woman's job to make sure that the help was looked after. You had to feed the men. If they were going to work after six in the evenings in the bright, they'd come into the house and have something to eat. You see the mill was the same. You only fed the main men and the mill and then the others would have their lunch outside. We'd make tea for them. That was the County Dublin way now. Oh the tea would come in to you too and you'd just heat it in teapots, big teapots.

Maureen Lawless

The steam engines and threshing mills were eventually replaced by combine harvesters which not only did the job quicker, but also meant that the farmer no longer had to wait for the threshing mill to come to his yard to do the job.

The combine harvester was a big development really because the farmers were able to get their own machinery. If it was nice and dry they'd cut it and if it was raining they'd stop. They were able to get out and get a fine day and cut an acre an hour. Thresh it and all, cut it and thresh it and then it went to a place where they had grain dryers. We had tractors in the last war, but then after that the combine harvesters came in. You'd stand up on it and you could go out to the field and cut it and bag it all in one go. The straw was on the ground so you used a pick up baler and it would be a tidy job.

Noel McAllister

The transition from steam to combustion powered rural machinery took Jack Harford with it as he moved from working on the land to selling the machines that farmers used to do the jobs which once he and his father had done.

We wouldn't go far wrong in describing Jack Harford of Cloughran as the ideal local character. There surely isn't a farmer in all North County Dublin that hasn't come across him at some time or another. In the war years his business boomed and Jack found himself investing in a variety of machinery. Farm mechanisation became almost a craze with him and he became a regular visitor at any Irish and English show where new implements were shown. His interest and knowledge in this field brought an offer from a Dublin tractor firm in 1946 that was tempting enough to persuade him to give up contracting altogether and switch from buying machines to selling them.

Irish Farmers Journal 10th March 1956

Each year in Fingal at harvest time the communal ties of all the farms were evident, as everybody in the community worked together, and this considerable co-operation between neighbours and friends was apparent throughout the year. Barter was the common form of payment for goods and services, whether it was for cures for sick animals or shop bought provisions. People were not working for financial gain, they were working for each other in their community, mutually dependent.

The local fellas, they'd have their cures now that the vet wouldn't. I don't know when they'd go for a vet, just when things were very bad. Basically it was the handyman, a herd. It'd be these men that'd come and do a lot of jobs with cattle. I suppose the farmer would know enough, but they'd always want the help of somebody else. Basically he was never paid. The way he was paid was a bag of rubbishy potatoes for the pigs, or hay or straw or something.

Maureen Lawless

It's like people didn't pay the shopkeeper at that time, not alone pay their neighbour. They would go to the local town and they would get the groceries and they would pay maybe with eggs or vegetables or butter and they would do an exchange with the grocer.

Simon Snow

This system extended to include Travellers who were welcome guests to farms in Fingal where they exchanged their skills as tinsmiths for farm produce.

You mean tinkers? They used to come in and out, there was quite a number of families, the Donovans, they'd arrive once or twice a year. They were brought into the parlour to sit down and they'd repair the pots and pans, bits and pieces. They were very respected Travellers. They'd probably put their wagon between fields along the road. They always respected property, they were always respected the Donovans. We'd go out to the pantry and take out pots and pans and say 'that one needs a repair'. They'd do a bit of work, take a few scraps and go off. They'd take water or milk and take a few potatoes, get a few spuds out of the shed.

Noel McAllister

As Fingal was urbanised and industrialisation was spreading, farms found a ready market for fresh produce in the local towns where money could be earned from the sale of eggs and butter and it was women who were expected to keep poultry and make the butter.

And of course we kept a couple of cows, and we churned and made butter and sold it locally in Swords, that you couldn't do now. I'd love to be doing that now, getting the fresh buttermilk. And all that had to stop, you see you were gettin' to different stages where things had to be modernised. Churnin' was a hard old chore twice a week but still and all it was nice to have the butter. And then of course we got the poultry and that was my job, then to do the eggs. We'd sell apples at the door cause we only had enough apples to. It wasn't commercial. It was more private and you'd have too much for yourself so we used to sell a lot. I started selling eggs in Swords. Like say there was Taylor's. Now they had a grocery shop and they used to take the eggs and they'd take the butter. That time you hadn't to worry about numbers or sizes or anything like that. You just brought in your eggs and they were sold there for you.

Maureen Lawless

I churned twice a week and made butter, sometimes we would have too much for ourselves, so we sold some, we did the same with eggs.

Miriam Arthurs

Women had always played an active role in the farming community in North County Dublin. They were a vital part of the workforce whether employed as agricultural labourers; the help, helping a farmer's wife to run a household or working on and managing their own farms. However, regardless of the role women played outside of the home they were expected to manage a rural home.

She (my mother) had to go out and work in the fields, and to rear us too. She'd go out in the morning, go out about 8 o'clock, come in and get her dinner at 12.30, then she'd be home for us getting in from school. She'd make dinner, maybe boil up a pot of spuds or maybe a stew the night before. She was a hard worker.

Peggy Reid who worked as a domestic servant.

Life was very hard them days. Women used to have to go out and pick potatoes and that. When they came home they had to wash clothes and mend clothes and do anything they had to. It wouldn't be big houses but just they had to keep them clean. There was seven of us. You used to have to go out and pick potatoes. There was no work, only in the fields that time.

Kitty Hughes who worked as a domestic servant.

Those who had farms of their own played an active part in the running of them, from looking after accounts to keeping poultry, in addition of course to the running of a rural home where drawing water, churning butter, baking bread and washing by hand were common household duties.

Light the range every morning and make the breakfast. It was a lot of hard work, and dirty work. I was always in trouble for being too particular. But you polished, come afternoon when you cleaned up, the next thing was you had to polish the grate, you know the range. There was a lot of work. And you had no rubber gloves in those days. Your poor old hands! I'll never forget.

Maureen Lawless

Just as it was common practice to employ a labourer on a farm, where it could be afforded it was usual to hire a girl to help the farmer's wife. Like the labourer who worked with and for the farmer, it was the girl's job to assist the farmer's wife in her work.

It was easy enough getting help those years. Sometimes they had to come from Swords, or maybe they'd live in. Yes there would be somebody helpin' out. There was girls down here and they'd come up yes, even when I was in Rathbeale. I always had a girl.

Maureen Lawless

The large crops, like potatoes, increasingly cultivated for the Dublin market provided a lot of employment because they were very labour intensive, as the crop had to be tended, picked and graded by hand and it was women who were often employed as labourers.

I had to work out in the fields when my husband died. My youngest was only five weeks old. So, I had to pick the potatoes, turnips, all different things. When we were thinning turnips or anything like that we had to get on our knees, or if we were pulling onions. But to dig potatoes we had big aprons hanging out of us. Mostly women (worked in the fields) and you didn't get it easy either.

Peggy Reid

Hard as it was, this type of work was an important source of extra income for rural families.

There could be up to six women from around the area this time of year (the autumn) picking potatoes and all that type of thing. And they'd leave their children in the headland and they'd go from one end of the evening to the other and the child would be left there. It was worth a few extra bob, the husband might be working as a ploughman or whatever he did and then the women might get this few months extra work.

Noel McAllister

Once the potatoes had been picked they had to be sorted before they could be sold to markets and shops in Dublin, and as with the picking this had to be done by hand.

Now they were higher than this house. Mountains of them, start here at the first and work your way through them.

Rose Canning, an agricultural labourer.

They'd be the big potatoes, talking about going back, even to my father's time, they were graded. The big potatoes went to the big shops. The hazards went to the poorer places. They were called hazards, they were small potatoes and they were given to pigs afterwards. But people, Moore Street and places like that would buy a certain amount of big ones but a certain amount of small ones as well and they'd do their own mixin'. And there might be a certain amount of potatoes left at the later end of it. Smaller potatoes, and that would be seed. They would grade them with their hands, down on the hands actually, down on their hands. There was no, I know there was a winnow for doing corn all right, but certainly there was nothing for grading potatoes that I knew of. They'd have a potato box and they put them into those and they'd be loaded up.

Maureen Lawless

Similarly women worked on the fruit farms and harvesting the corn.

And of course the corn harvest and the saving of the hay too, provided their fair share of work for men and women alike. We used to go out in the harvest then. Help stack up the corn. And four of them used to go up on the hay, make the hay.

Kitty Hughes

From 35 to 40 men with three tractors, seven horses and a very wide range of machinery are employed regularly, while 40 to 45 women and girls are busy weeding for eight or nine months each year. Most of the men are either local or from Lusk, while the majority of women and girls are from the Swords area. During the fruit picking season of about two months, an extra 250-300 people are employed, drawn from the surrounding area as far as Santry on the one side and Balbriggan on the other.

February 1943, The Fingal Fingerpost

They (the men) would be out this time of year you know. They would be cutting the meadow and all and I used to love it and I would be out there throwing hay with them.

Rose Canning

Fruit picking was physically demanding work. As soon as the fruit was ripe it had to be brought in, because it could not be allowed to go unpicked for too long as it would rot and this allied with the demands of the markets in Dublin meant that the pickers had to work long hours.

If we were picking, we'd have to be in at 8 o'clock in the morning and you'd have your lunch at twelve for a half hour, and then you'd go out to work again until six. Thirteen shillings and nine pence you got for the week. The pay wasn't very good at that time, work wasn't dear. Crowds working, coming from Dublin and everywhere to work in it. I used to cycle over to Scotts (the fruit farm) in fact, and if the bike was punctured I'd walk it and that's a few miles out. Now in the summer, on a Monday morning, you'd be picking for the market and you'd have to be in there at five o'clock in the morning, work all day then until nine, and then you'd have your break and work till twelve and then till six again. June now, the fruit would be coming in, you know, June and July and August and then the gooseberries out in the orchard. Oh it was great in Scotts out in the sun, your brain would be pounding. You know you'd be burnt alive and then you'd go down on one knee. I have rheumatism in my knee, that's where I got it.

Rose Canning

A woman's working experience of farming in Fingal in this period very much depended on her social status. On the more affluent farms, it was accepted that a farmer's wife did not work outdoors in the fields, but for the majority of women the prevailing economic climate meant that they had no real choice but to do agricultural work to help support their families.

It was more or less a feminine thing, looking after the house end. It was my experience of not really going out to the fields to do anything. It was a woman's job to make sure that the help was looked after, you had to feed men and things like that.

Maureen Lawless

I worked in them for, it must have been for over twenty years, working in the fields, weeding, picking potatoes and doing all sorts of things, you know on the farm. I loved it, I loved the outside work.

Rose Canning

 One of the most àrduous tasks women had to do on a farm was to draw water everyday for household use. Prior to rural electrification farms had to rely upon natural sources of water, water mains being limited to urbanised areas and it was the coming of electricity which facilitated the introduction of electric pumps. Women were petitioned and encouraged to advocate that their farms were attached to the electrical supply by both the Electricity Supply Board (ESB) and organisations such as The Irish Countrywomen's Association (ICA).

Young ladies of the country; make it known that there will be no more marriages until there is hot and cold water on tap in the kitchen.

James Dillon, Minister for Agriculture
ICA Annual Fair, Dublin, 8th November 1950.

The long low thatched building, with the well a field or two away and the candle in the window at nightfall - all that might be something for the homesick Yankees to enthuse over, but it was heartbreak for the unfortunate woman who had to keep it clean. It was she who had to tramp the mucky path to the well, and carry back every bucket of water needed for her work.

Mary Purcell speaking at Ladies Day, Muintir na Tíre Rural Week 1959.

It had not been until the end of World War II that a concerted effort was made to supply rural Ireland with electricity. The ESB had been created in 1927 to operate, manage and develop Ireland's electricity network and prior to the building of the hydroelectric generator at Ardnacrusha on the Shannon, there had been over three hundred independent suppliers in the country. They were predominantly in urban areas and had to rely on imported coal to power their generators.

> *Old Flanagan was a great man, he had electricity running in Skerries when there was electricity nowhere. He had two big German machines there, pumping, pumping day and night. And he had hot water baths, a skating rink and everything there on the side. He had power in Skerries, street lights. Skerries was the only station that had electricity on the line between, well Drogheda had, Dublin had gas. Skerries town had the electricity poles in it, all run by Flanagan. I believe he charged a shilling a unit and that was the way he charged. Not every house had it, any house that could afford to have it, had it. He had the lorries every other week, you'd see him going down with a big load of coal. They pumped day and night.*

Larry McNally, who worked on the railways in Fingal.

The Shannon Scheme meant that the electricity network was rationalised under the auspices of one supplier and by 1929 the electricity supply was available in the more urbanised parts of Fingal such as Balbriggan, Malahide and Swords.

> *Oh, we had electricity, the Shannon Scheme had been in operation from the late 20's, we had that. In 1937 my family built what now stands the Sands Hotel, the Portmarnock Hotel, there was no shortage of electricity then. The electric line came from, out from Dublin.*

Patsy Magill, who owned a cinema and dancehall in Malahide.

The availability of electricity in rural Ireland was limited and obviously this had a profound effect on working and living conditions and on the instructions of Seán Lemass in 1942 the ESB was told to draw up plans for the introduction of electricity to the rest of the country. At the time their plans were seen as audacious given the fact that Ireland was economically isolated because of World War II, however it was the Emergency which had illustrated how weak Ireland's infrastructure was and the urgent need to modernise the country.

In our country electrification is more than merely producing light and power; it is bringing light into darkness. If we do that, we will have brought a new outlook to many of these people. If we can get them light and nothing else, then I think we have brought about a great change.

James Larkin T.D., Dáil Éireann 24th January, 1945

The first village in Ireland to be electrified under the Rural Electrification Scheme (RES) was Oldtown, North County Dublin on the 15th January, 1947. The ESB created a dedicated organisation, the Rural Electrical Office (REO) to oversee and implement their policy and as well as bringing electricity to rural Ireland they brought much needed employment as in each area a gang of up to a hundred men would be employed to work on installation.

The rural electrification, that was a wonderful thing altogether. Wonderful, the amount of work it gave at the time too, unemployment was bad at that time, as it is now. It gave work all over the country, digging and sinking these poles down and putting the cable up.

Jim Hall, a soldier in the Irish Army.

The REO adopted existing Catholic parishes as the territorial unit they would operate in, and were quick to utilise existing parish organisations such as parish councils and Emergency committees to help with the introduction of electricity into each area. Each parish would be shown the benefits of electricity by a Rural Electrification Committee and Area Organiser, who would set up demonstrations and meetings for potential customers. Once people were convinced of the advantages of electricity they would be signed up for installation.

There was a circular sent around all the houses and people were given a choice to take it or not. There was a certain amount of cost involved, that was the big snag; you had people who didn't have the money in those days. Well they found that the majority of people wanted it and the town was notified, so it was in. Because it was cheaper in the long run to wire a street rather than wire one here and one there. Eventually people were persuaded that they would have to take in electricity anyway.

Jack Buckley, a dance band musician.

The problem here for the REO was 'backsliders', people who would agree to take electricity, but then would decide against it in the time between signing up and the electricity being connected. Their withdrawal obviously affected the economic viability of an area and could mean delays in the area being connected. One of the main problems was with smaller farms, where farmers were worried about having to make regular cash payments. Consumers at this time were charged a fixed rate irrespective of the use they made of the service and this type of system was certainly outside of the farming tradition where income was at best irregular. The other problem the REO faced was rural people's suspicion and mistrust of electricity. Some regarded it as a luxury which their life-style did not warrant and others regarded it as a dangerous invention.

> *There was one room in the house which was Paddy's room and he wouldn't have it in there and we had this one room on the house which didn't have electricity. And when he went to hospital and I was given this room and I had to use a candle. I think they thought it would go on fire. Especially people with thatched houses, (they) were afraid to get it in because they were afraid it'd go on fire, but when you think about it the oil lamps were probably more dangerous. I remember using candles all right and an oil lamp and it gave pretty good light.*

Bernadette Marks, a local historian.

However for the people who did subscribe to the electrical supply, it brought immediate changes and benefits to their working life on farms.

> *It was a great advantage to farming people. The introduction, say of the milking machine when the electricity came in cut away a lot of the hand machines. It also had a lot of advantages in other ways, people used it to grind their own corn, light for the farm yard.*

Simon Snow

> *It showed up all the houses! That was in the 40's sometime, the electricity came. It was wonderful! You know you were pumping water, dragging water (before it was connected), it was a wonderful thing to get into the farm (to) pump your water. Then the toilets of course started. You had lights, outside lights were a great asset because this time of year (the winter), now the farmers would be going out at night. They'd have to light a lamp to feed their horses for the next morning. You must remember they left the farm at 4 o'clock in the morning to go into the Dublin market with their cabbage.*

Maureen Lawless

The changes experienced by the men and women who worked on farms in this period in Fingal saw farming methods revolutionised. Each new wave of modernisation brought increasing pressure for farming to become practiced as a business as opposed to the continuation of traditional working life. Whilst it was welcomed where it alleviated the hardships of working a farm, it meant that a traditional way of life was relegated to the annals of folklore as agriculture increasingly became agribusiness.

> *I was real sad the day my son went to Warrenstown and he came back and said it's time now, the cows job was over. The cattle were taking up too many sheds. But that part was over and you were sad for it in a way. I saw three generations growing potatoes; my father, my husband and then my son. I think that they let things get too big. You know like you have to be big now to be in potatoes. The machinery is so expensive that people have to stay put in it to get the cost of their stuff.*

Maureen Lawless

THE BLACKSMITH

Everybody had to use horses. Milkmen had to use horses, every delivery, coal deliveries, most deliveries to the shops, all had horse-drawn trailers. All the farms and race-courses around this area. Every farm had a cart for transporting people from one town or another, there was no buses.

Pat French, a blacksmith still working in Baldoyle.

I came here and I built this (the forge) and started up then in opposition to seven or eight blacksmiths in this area. It was a terrible area for blacksmiths at that time. Well, like it was all horse-shoeing, doing farm implements. Well, now it's electric welding that they're done with you see, years ago it used to be welding in the fire. Well the real blacksmith worked you know, taking up one of them bars of iron and making things out of it. See it used to be making horseshoes. Well now you get them machine-made shoes. I used to make shoes here, then the machine-made shoes came in and they were cheaper but, they wasn't as good.

Bill Casey, a blacksmith still working in Bog O' the Ring.

The blacksmith and his craft had a special place in rural communities, for his work combined not only great strength and finesse, but skills which were vital to an agricultural society. His trade was peculiar as it combined the social standing of a doctor or teacher with hard, physical labour. The way their craft has changed is closely linked to the way rural Ireland has changed, as both technology and custom have irrevocably impinged on the work practices and social standing of smiths.

Unlike farriers who worked exclusively with horses the blacksmith worked for and with everybody in the community who needed his skills.

Shoeing cartwheels, putting hooks on cartwheels and building harrows and repairing ploughs and field-gates and making a gate. I would often have to make up grubbers and things them years. (They were) for doing drills of potatoes and turnips. Hunter hoes some of them called them. And old ploughs, made a few harrows in our time. Well the carpenter used to go (working with the blacksmith), making carts and wheels and running jobs around the farm yard, doors and things like that. The blacksmith had to make the mountings for those jobs, the iron stays and a few of the wheels, make door mountings, hinges and that for the doors. But where I was, there was all kinds of job work a doing. You know there was, working for old farms and factories around Drogheda.

Bill Casey

A blacksmith's work was steady all year round and like all rural trades, the seasons and elements played their part in dictating the level of activity around the forge.

No such things as 'day-offs'. Not really when you are at this racket, you know, because someone will come down and the world will be at an end if you're not there. In real good weather now, in springtime, you mightn't think of a day off.

Bill Casey

The forge was a great source of income in the years following the Emergency and farmers, like the rest of the rural community, would often tender payment in kind.

Ah yes, in Swords. There were two brothers (both blacksmiths), the two Donnellys. One was Mick and the other was Matt I think. Two brothers anyway, and they never spoke. Never spoke. And whoever you went to, the (other) brother wouldn't talk to you. Mick was the fellow we went to. That was a big day, off into Swords then and to get him into good form you'd have to go over to the shop and get him a few pints. He was a good blacksmith, fair dues.

Maureen Lawless

There was a lot of one and six pences and half crown jobs them years 'cos them you were working for hadn't money. But then if you wanted a bag of potatoes or something like that you had no bother getting them. Some of them like they'd kill a pig for their own use and if you were knocking about the place they'd give you a lump of bacon. But you'd be blasted with salt, you know, home cure.

Bill Casey

The practice of barter also extended to local shop-keepers and it was rare for money to be paid to blacksmiths for the work they did.

I know that little blacksmith that was down there, Dick Lacey. Dick'd come up for his groceries (to McAnally's shop) and there was a balance one time of a couple of shillings. Nancy McAnally squared up and Nancy owed him two or three shillings, whatever it was that time. The shop, there was four or five men in it and Dick Lacey turned around to some of them, says he 'That's the first time I ever got money across the counter!', and him working for them so long. Whatever he'd do would be worked out of it.

Bill Casey

Saving the hay at Dublin Airport at the end of the Emergency

An Aer Lingus DC3 being refuelled by Shell and BP in the late 1940's.

The Hill of Howth Tram at Baily Post Office

Jack Harford driving a steam engine taking an electricity generator from the North Wall to Poulaphouca

Eamonn Lawless of Swords ploughing in the late 1940's

Eamonn Lawless of Swords planting potatoes

The Dye House at Smyth's Hosiery Factory, Balbriggan

Women working in Smyth's Hosiery Factory, Balbriggan

FRONT COVER PHOTOGRAPH:

Front cover and details of the back cover are of Jack Harford's Threshing Mill and Steam Engine

---

Economic frugality also extended to the blacksmith's raw material which was iron, and he would be given scrap to recycle. However this practice didn't always meet with the approval of those working the forge.

Sometimes if a fella maybe had cart hoops lying about the yard he'd say 'I must bring you over those few hoops make a few sets of shoes.' But then he'd be expecting one or two sets free for the iron. We very seldom split up cart hoops, too much bother with them. Men had no money of course to buy iron that time.

Bill Casey

During World War II when every available resource of iron and steel was being utilised for the production of armaments in Europe and there was little in the way of imports to Ireland, blacksmiths had no choice but to rely upon scrap metal for their work.

They (horse shoes) were made from scrap steel during the War when there was no steel, you used to make them out of iron from beds, bedsteads. You couldn't get the steel you had to go around the farms and fields and take iron from the gaps in the hedges. The young lads home from school would be sent out and around to collect all the iron and bring it in and they'd melt it down in the fire.

Pat French

The end of the war saw more and more Irish farmers starting to replace horses with tractors, but this in no way heralded an end to the smith's working relationship with farms. Machinery, such as ploughs or harrows, which had been designed for horses was now being used with tractors and this created work for blacksmiths.

They were very light tractors, they were Massey-Fergusons, they were only twenty horsepower. Still they were a hell of a lot more powerful than two horses. A lot of the parts on these things (horse-drawn machinery) were just cast, broke very easily, especially the ploughs with just cast tips on them. And when they hit a rock they were in bits. Horse machinery was never made for tractors at all. Well, if you weren't able to fix it you went to the forge, the local blacksmith, Connell was his name. He looked after the horses too and he repaired you know, if a machine broke. If not, you had to go to the distributors.

Noel McAllister

Before the advent of mobile forges, as used by many farriers today, the very physicality of the forge had a profound effect on the store of myth and folklore surrounding its presence and place in rural communities. Everyday objects were imbued with a mysticism that ranged from the mundane to the fantastic. The forge water, used to cool the metals being worked, was reputed to be charged with curative properties for removing warts, a remedy which had mixed results.

The forge water, for curing warts? If you were heating say the likes of these (forge tongs) from morning and when they're red hot you just get them and dip them in water. A school teacher years ago used to send kids from school to cure warts.

Pat French

A blacksmith was supposed to have a cure for warts. He used to cool the horseshoes and the irons in the tub. But, I had a wart and I used to put it into the water now and again, but it didn't work.

Bill Casey

The anvil and the sonorous tones that rang out as a piece of metal was being worked on it came to be acknowledged as the source of the tuning of the fiddle and it was said that you could tell what was being worked on from the sound of the hammer blows.

It used to be when fellas would be working years ago in the fields, 'Oh, Dick Lacey's shoeing horses.' They'd know with the sound of the anvil what he'd be doing. Them years they were used to the sound and the noise, because they were after seeing him, they'd know every sound, they'd know every sound what he was doing with the shoe.

Bill Casey

The forge was also a natural focal point for men to gather, not only was it warm and dry but there was the added attraction of watching a smith at work.

It used to be a wet day, there'd be two or three horses to be shod and a lad would come maybe on a bicycle just to put in the time. A wet day was a recognised day in a forge. They had meetings here, about certain things, cricket meetings and things like that. Balrothery had a great cricket team. Balbriggan, they had a good team, a couple of good teams.

Bill Casey

In winter, the residual warmth in the forge meant it was an attractive place patronised by men after a day's work.

It used to be a great meeting place, you see the heat would be in the place from the day's work. They used to play cards here at night after work, they'd go to the local pub, get a few bottles of the local malt, bring it back and there'd be a card session. Ah, they used to spend ages here. In fact, there was a man here, I believe he was kind of homeless and he used to sleep here at night.

Pat French

The traditional skills employed by blacksmiths have declined with the advent of welding and smiths feel that with the passing of their skills the quality of the work done has similarly fallen off.

Yes, them years the old farmers were very particular. You had to do the right thing for them. Any of them that's at it now, they're just cutting pieces with an angle-grinder and welding it up. There's no great skill involved.

Bill Casey

There is a modern way to do things now, modern machinery, and it's quicker ways of doing the same job. It's quicker and there's less time involved, time meant nothing years ago.

Pat French

DOMESTIC SERVICE

Despite the fact that the numbers employed in domestic service began to decrease from the beginning of the century there were still many houses in Fingal in the 1930's and 1940's which had their own parlour maids, housekeepers and cooks. The majority of these were women and many of them came to Dublin from the country to take up 'situations' with middle class families. Servants were a symbol of status for any affluent family. Employers ranged from doctors and clergy to lawyers, members of government and business people.

> *I worked with all country girls, you know. I very seldom worked with a Dublin person. You know Dublin people had factories and they went to factories. You know you had Lemons and there was a lot of factories around that they went into. So it was all country people that worked in the houses.*
>
> **Bridget Whelan, who worked as a domestic servant.**

The work of the servant varied from house to house, depending on the number of servants employed. While only the very wealthy could afford a butler, a chauffeur, a housekeeper, a cook, a parlourmaid and a charlady or scullery maid, there were also many houses which employed one or two servants. Jenny Graham's experience was in Turvey House where she was one of three servants, while Bridget Whelan worked on her own and combined the duties of cleaner, cook and childminder.

> *There was a cook, I was parlour maid. So, I brought up all the meals and cleared away; set the tables. Didn't do any rough work, (the charlady) came in and done the washing and scrubbing.*
>
> **Jenny Graham, who worked as a domestic servant.**

You had a routine. You got into a routine. And it was a routine that was very hard to break. It still stayed with me and now I'm what, 64 or 65. You got up between seven and eight and you started doing the breakfast, you done the fire and you generally had porridge during Lent and after Lent they had a nice fry. It was a completely different organisation altogether. You done your washing by rubbing the board and there was no carpets so every room had to be swept on a Tuesday and then on Thursday you done the other quarter of the house where you had a sitting room, dining room and if they entertained you had to look after them. With the result that you had to wear a uniform. That was the kind of thing you did. If they had a party, you had to look after the guests and wash up. There was no such thing as washing machines, you were doing all the washing by hand.

Bridget Whelan

Domestic servants worked without the aid of labour-saving devices but instead were well acquainted with the simple elements of water, heat and physical energy.

You used to put on the whites to boil in a big black pot on the fire. They were all done on Sunday evening. Then you washed them out on the next morning, Monday morning.

Jenny Graham

Etiquette was all important in the life of the 'Big House' and the hierarchy of employer to servant was well respected. This sense of hierarchy extended to the servants themselves where the housekeeper, butler and cook were held in higher regard than the other servants. Generally, each servant had a clear idea of their own position, status and duties and were aware of the behaviour expected of them.

You didn't, I mean there was things you didn't do. For instance if they were eating, you couldn't go into the room, and you didn't eat with them. You always ate in the kitchen. That was one of the things. You could not go into a room without knocking at the door. To the present day, I couldn't go into a room without knocking at the door and you'd get all those things instilled into you when you were younger, and if they were going out you couldn't go with them, you know. If you were going out and they were going out, you couldn't both go the one way. No, they didn't associate with the servants. I mean you were a servant and that was it, that was your life. You just went on from there.

Bridget Whelan

In houses where there was no cook employed, the 'domestic' was responsible for the preparation of everyday meals. However, when her employer was entertaining she took on a different role and was expected to behave in a stately and courteous fashion.

You always brought them breakfast in bed. You brought the wife breakfast in bed whatever she wanted. Like, brought up the tray. It was generally plain cooking, there was never anything very fancy. If there was something very fancy she would do it herself. You know, you done plain cooking. You done bacon and cabbage or you done a vegetable, potatoes, and you done meat you know. But there were no desserts. There was just plain wholesome food. If they were entertaining she would do the cooking. She'd tell you to watch it all right, you know. She'd have you there kind of looking after the thing. And then you'd have to put on a black frock and a white apron and a white hat in your hair, a little gadget like that, you just walked by them (the guests). You didn't associate with those sort of people.

Bridget Whelan

As the domestic servant received free bed and board, her pay was generally more like pocket money than an actual wage. Due to the nature of her work and her live-in circumstances she also had little time off. Her work started around 7 a.m. with the lighting of the stove and the preparation of the breakfast and continued until at least 7 p.m. when the supper was over and she had cleaned up. Because she lived in the house she was always under the authority of her master or mistress and always 'on call' for whatever duties that may have arisen.

I remember one place when we were getting paid by the month. We were getting a fiver a month. In the late 40's, early 50's. But then you see you got your board, so you didn't have to pay for that. And you were fed. And you generally got good food. I must say that about them. Everyone fed you to the best. Well if you got time off you brought the kids for a walk. That was your time off, yeah. Well looking back I don't even think of these things. Once you start talking about them you know. Well, that's it. You got one day off a week. But then you had a night off which was your night off and now they would not dream of taking that day or night off you. That was your night off and you got that. You went off and you enjoyed yourself, you know.

Bridget Whelan

There was no standard rate of payment for domestic workers. The Irish Women Workers' Union attempted between 1912 and 1941 to obtain better conditions of employment for domestic servants. Helena Moloney, and later Mrs. Buckley worked as General Secretaries of the Domestic Workers' Union and sought salary increases, sick pay, minimum notice, references, bonuses and overtime for servants. In June 1941 they made the decision to abandon their attempts as they had failed to organise domestic servants together. Their problem was largely due to the isolation of servants from each other.

> *I wasn't as keen on housework because with the hospitals (working in the hospitals) you had more company than you would if you were working in a house on your own, you were kind of isolated, you know. You'd probably have a room up in the attic. But, they were all big houses. Some of them were very big houses, maybe three or four stories up. You know and you'd have this little tiny pokey thing up in the attic and that was your quarters.*

Bridget Whelan

Courtship or marriage were neither facilitated or accepted in the life of the domestic servant. Employees were often dissuaded from having 'followers'. Women were limited in the number of prospective male partners that they encountered and as a result many tended to marry the milkmen, breadmen, butchers, roundsmen or local shopkeepers.

> *I worked in another place too. She was a doctor's wife. Any case, this morning it was a Monday morning, I left at 10 a.m. in the morning and left her in the lurch; the messenger boy came out for the order at 9 o'clock in the morning and I asked her what she wanted, she came out and she said 'What are you doing there flirting with the messenger boy?', 'I beg your pardon' says I 'I'm not flirting.' 'Go down and get my breakfast' she says. She insulted me and I said to her 'I didn't say anything'. Down I goes and got my shoes and polished them and all like that, she rang the bell again, she rang again and out she comes and she says 'I rang for my breakfast'. I said 'well if you want your breakfast you can cook it yourself! I'm going!'*

Peggy Reid, who worked as a domestic servant.

Women were expected to be one hundred percent loyal to their employers, yet on marrying, they were required to give up work.

No, it wasn't the done thing, a married woman working. It's amazing now you see all the young married women going out working. They just didn't do it. You got older women all right that had their family reared and they would get a menial job. It was just scrubbing floors. Now that's all they could get 'cause that's all they were fit for. At that stage that's what everyone thought. It really was a man's world, in the '40's and '50s. The last man I worked for, it was up in what's it ... Grace ... oh! Grace something in or around Whitehall and I only stuck him for a week. Then he discovered I was married, and that didn't go down too well at all. Women didn't work when they got married. No, that wasn't the done thing. No, once you got married you were out of a job. I mean, honestly speaking, you get married and you were in a job, you were out immediately. You might get a bit of holiday money going, but, that was it. No, you didn't go back to work. So, when I went back to work I had to use my maiden name. So when he found out I was married he sacked me.

Bridget Whelan

Up until the end of the 1950's domestic servants were still being employed but since the end of the war their numbers had been rapidly declining. This was due to a number of factors, not least the realisation amongst women that there was better paid work available. The impact of emigration and an increased awareness of emancipation meant that women were no longer prepared to work as domestic servants. Nowhere was this more apparent than in newspapers where it was the employers who now advertised positions and not domestic servants seeking employment.

DOMESTIC SERVANTS WANTED
COOK – General, for Doctor's house; must be experienced; references essential; wages 25s - 30s. Mrs. Jennings, Park View, Whitehall, Dublin.

Irish Independent, 18th September, 1947.

WANTED – steady Girl, good plain cook and bread-maker; 30/- weekly indoor; state age, send copies. Box 1080.

Irish Independent 19th September 1947.

THE EMERGENCY AND WORKING LIFE

What You Should do to Protect Your Country in the Event of Invasion by a Foreign Power ...
- Don't hinder the Army by crowding roads, or hampering operations, but do everything to help.
- Don't co-operate with, or assist the enemy.
- Assist your neighbours.
- Keep a stout heart! Don't believe rumours and don't help spread them.

Department of Defence, Public Information, Pamphlet No. 1

The hardest years that I ever remember was during the war years, there was very little of anything.

Kitty Hughes

The outbreak of World War II and the policy of neutrality the Republic adopted had a profound effect on working life in Ireland. Whilst Ireland's neutrality saved the country from the horrors of war, Ireland suffered economically because of its isolation and, being a non-combatant, it had none of the advantages of a war-time economy. As the war in Europe progressed imports to Ireland became increasingly rare forcing the country to forget all notions of economic development. Instead, the paramount need was to secure a high degree of economic self-sufficiency. Both Irish industry and agriculture suffered in this period. There was little industrial development due to the shortages of raw materials and machinery and similarly as Emergency farming was basically subsistence farming, agricultural development was also hindered throughout the war period. Emigration remained high in this period with Irish men and women working in Britain's war production factories and serving in the British armed forces, and by 1945 it was estimated that there was some 50,000 people from Ireland serving in the British forces. The Irish Army was an important source of employment in this period and at its peak, its strength had risen from 7,500 to 38,000 regulars. The declaration of neutrality meant that the role of the army was a defensive one, observing and protecting the country's borders against the possibility of invasion from either Britain or Germany. Certainly in 1939 Churchill, then First Lord of the Admiralty, had brought considerable pressure to bear on the British government to demand the use of naval facilities in Ireland and if they were not forthcoming to take them by force. Equally it is true that whilst Germany had considered and ruled out invading Ireland and then attempting to invade Britain, if Britain had been taken in 1940 there were contingency plans to carry the invasion over into the Republic. (Ireland Since the Famine, Lyons, pp. 555-556). These fears of invasion were heightened when German bombs were dropped on Dublin in the early years of the war.

There was the big threat of invasion in 1940, that the Germans were going to invade and the Jews had the awful fear, but we didn't realise that if they did, it would be curtains for them. So when the two houses that were Jewish houses on the South Circular Road were bombed we thought it was, that the Germans had learned that the Jews were there.

Kitty Hayes, who worked in the Civil Service.

Ireland was not quite as secure as she thought according to a report in the German newspaper 'National Zeitung' written by a Naval commander on the progress of the war, not only would the English Channel soon be under German control but 'even the Irish Sea and Éire are already within the German reach.'

The Irish Independent, 28th May 1940.

As well as the local Defence Forces (LDF), who acted in a voluntary capacity, the army's ranks were bolstered by what were known as 'Emergency Men', who joined up as full-time soldiers.

The fellows who joined the army joined as Emergency Men. Now a lot of firms the men were working with made up their pay from thirteen and tuppence to what they were having in their jobs. Now, for instance, we had a lot of prison warders who joined us; now of course they were government employees too. Their wages were made up to what they were as prison wardens while they were in the army, turf workers, another one. A lot of civil servants joined up too; Revenue we had quite a lot of them.

Jim Hall, a member of the Irish Army from 1930 to 1952.

But for many recruits the wage remained 'thirteen and tuppence' a week and this, coupled with the prevailing economic situation meant that in spite of the war Irish people were still emigrating. Since the 1930's when America had started to control the number of immigrants it received through visas and quotas, most emigrants had gone to work and live in Britain and this remained true throughout the Emergency period. Many Irish men and women contributed to Britain's war effort working in factories or by joining the British Army. Once again it was economic necessity, given the lack of opportunities in Ireland, that forced people to emigrate.

Well there wasn't any work here like at the time and I'd either join the British Army or the army here. But I wanted to see fresh fields like you know, and a number of us joined for that reason.

Maurice Hartigan who left Dublin at the beginning of World War II to join the British Army.

Well, we had an awful lot of young fellas joined at the beginning of the Emergency and they became disillusioned with the Irish army, particularly the low wages, thirteen and tuppence a week. They became disillusioned and they thought the British army were going off to fight in Spain and France instead of the green fields of Ireland. They thought that was more attractive than soldiering on in the Irish army and they deserted. But a lot of them were heavily punished when they came back. Arbour Hill was full of deserters, when they came back on holidays there were military police at ports and stations and they would pick them up. There was bound to be a section getting disillusioned; the pay was bad and the work was hard.

Jim Hall

The British army was not only a source of employment for Irish men but also a source of income for their families back home.

They'd make an allowance for their families, they'd get marriage allowance, they'd have a book from the post office.

Maurice Hartigan

The British army had a different system, if you were married you were put in the family establishment and you got marriage allowance.

Jim Hall

So, although the men were fighting for the British army, their families were still provided for. Irish emigrants also found work in Britain's war industries, and bolstered their families incomes by sending money home.

Well they worked at ship-building and building of aerodromes and all like that you know, all that type of work: navvying and munitions.

Maurice Hartigan

Sure there was no other thing for them, there was a lot of women who left this country to go to England to work in munitions and all that. I've a sister now, she has a pension, a British pension for her services in the munitions during the war.

Jim Hall

Emigrants' remittances received in Eire last year totalled £8,379,000 compared with £3,103,000 in 1938 and £3,857,000 in 1941. Remittances from Britain rose from £600,000 in 1938 to £6,800,000 in 1942.

The Irish Independent, 13th October 1943

Throughout the war, mail was censored by both the Irish and British governments.

It was my job of censoring letters, a hundred a day during the war. You see letters were opened, not all of them, but at random. You'd get your bundle and you had to read a hundred.

Kitty Hayes

The vigilance and suspicion of both governments meant that letter writers were by necessity circumspect about what they wrote.

But you wouldn't put down a hell of a lot like, you had to be careful what you put down in your letters.

Maurice Hartigan

Although anything which would compromise Irish or British security was struck from the letter, enclosed money was carefully handled.

Anything subversive at all, there was a list like and you had to watch for them. Now if money was enclosed you had to pin it to the letter and hand it up to the staff officer. You had to be very careful because a lot of husbands were working in England at the time and they used to be sending money home to their wives.

Kitty Hayes

In fact there was an awful lot of money sent back, from America to the parents. Fabulous sense of belonging and responsibility. They went to make a good living and when they got work they sent back the dollars in fair numbers.

Jack Buckley

In stark contrast to the types of mail the Irish received was the style of letter they sent to family and friends abroad.

We used to like the American letters, they used to send photographs and we used to love going through all the photographs. And then the Irish ones to America were real tales of woe telling 'things were so hard with the rationing and poor father was drinking with tears running down his cheeks and the cow had broken her leg' and it was usually a tale of woe to America from which we were getting money.

Kitty Hayes

Ireland's standing army of regulars and reserves was bolstered by some 17,000 volunteers who were organised into the Local Defence Force (LDF), civilians trained to act as the vanguard in the event of an invasion.

'Not only for the present, but for a long time afterwards, we will need the manhood of the country to be trained as they are at present in the volunteer forces, it may be necessary for the existence of this nation that compulsory service will be introduced.' So declared Mr. de Valera at a march-past of the North Louth defence forces in Dundalk yesterday.

The Irish Times 13th September 1943

The principle was, that if there was an invasion of the country the LDF were the first men in the front line. Now they were supposed to offer a little stop-block until the army was fully organised and equipped to proceed to where the invasion happened.

Jim Hall

Like so many post-colonial institutions in Ireland, the army had the legacy of the British administration to deal with, following independence. In the thirties Irish soldiers were still being trained by British men serving in the Republic's army.

We trained for three months in the Curragh. We were under a lot of ex-British army sergeants and British army instructors, and they thought they were still in the British army. They were all given ranks to entice them to keep in the Irish army. When they were dealing with Irish men, well there was a bit of a divergence of opinion between us and the crowd that was training us. They used to treat us as they would British army recruits. Now, of course they were the hardest men in the British army.

Jim Hall

However as neutrality threw Ireland into isolation it meant that not only was the country forced to be self-reliant, but it also helped to unify the country as a whole and lay to rest some of the ghosts of the country's colonial past.

Now I came across a peculiar situation in Dundalk. There was two sections (of the LDF); one was dead IRA Republican and the other was British to the core, led by Colonel Kearns of Kearn's Brewery. Now he was the man who was leading the pro-British element down there. But the other crowd, they were red hot Republicans and they hated Colonel Kearns. If they had come to a show-down they would have been at each other's throats.

Jim Hall

This particular problem in Dundalk was solved by the 'promotion' of Kearns up to Belfast.

The following week Colonel Kearns was shifted from in charge of the group in Dundalk and Julianstown and he had some petty job in Belfast supervising the defence of Belfast, supervising civilian defence, but he was shifted anyhow.

Jim Hall

The only things that matched the fervour of the men who joined the LDF was the lack of resources and experience they had and it was the job of the regular army to instruct them into the basic skills of soldiering and to impart to them a sense of martial discipline.

Well we had to train the LDF and we made the LDF in no uncertain terms (aware of) their duties when we were giving them lectures. Some of them were enthusiastic enough about it. For instance now I was sent from Gormanstown to take a group of LDF in Swords. Now, I went out to the Sluagh Hall in Swords, there was three or four hundred men there. And all very keen and anxious but, no equipment, no nothing. So I took them on anyhow and I made them into sections and appointed section leaders. And they were responsible to me then for the roll call and the attendance and you had to make a return when I went back to camp. And I had another one in Malahide and they were equally as bad and as enthusiastic.

Jim Hall

The basic shortages of equipment and machinery which faced the whole country were also faced by the Irish army and the volunteer forces but they were clandestinely solved by the British army.

It was smuggled with the eyes open. Well now, I'm going to tell you something. What we got from across the border, we'd never have equipped the army only for what we got across the border. It wasn't generally known, it wasn't publicly known at the time, but there was convoys of lorries went from here to Crossmaglen and other little British outposts along the border. They went under cover of darkness and they came back under the cover of darkness, but they came back loaded with what the British that time had; old 303 Lee Enfield rifles. There were hundreds and thousands of those things sent from the border down to us from the British Armory. It was an arrangement they had made, they made the case that we couldn't maintain our neutrality and that anyone who wanted to come in, they could come in to any port around the coast if we had nothing to prevent them from coming in. De Valera was as much co-operating with the British army as anyone although he declared neutrality. But, it was the British army he was co-operating with, but he was benefitting by co-operating.

Jim Hall

Throughout the Emergency the LDF were active in a sentinel role; patrolling, guarding important installations and maintaining their readiness via continuous training and exercises both locally and for two weeks at annual training camps.

Just the basics, well initially before they got rifles and things, foot drill was all we could give them; form fours and square drill. But they enjoyed it, because they were doing something, because they all got the idea they were doing something for the country and it was up to us to imbue them with that spirit.

Jim Hall

A volunteer fire service was also started as part of the country's defences and this service was carried on once the war ended using military equipment.

It was first set up during the war in 1941, as a voluntary service, no pay. In the 1950's, when the war was over a lot of us carried on for nothing, we weren't paid. We did it for the people of Fingal. It was army equipment we had at that time. In the 50's the County Council took it over and they made it a retained Fire Service. We all had other jobs. We were carpenters and plumbers and lorry-drivers and builder's labourers and farmer's labourers, we had everything.

Joe O'Rourke who was a Fire Officer at Dublin Airport and a volunteer in the Fire Service.

In 1946, with the war over, the army stepped down from its emergency footing and the LDF was disbanded and replaced with the FCA, An Forsa Cosanta Áitiúil. But the end of the Emergency did not mean a return to pre-war life. Five years of rationing had taken its toll on the nation's health and tuberculosis had reached epidemic proportions. One of the dominant memories people have of the Emergency years is of the poor quality of food. Food rationing affected everyone in Irish society and many of the solutions to food shortages were relatively unpalatable. Farmers were compelled to grow more corn because of the Compulsory Tillage Order however, imported fertilizers were no longer available and farmers had to rely on organic manure and rock phosphate from County Clare. Not only did the amount of grain produced decrease, but the quality of the Irish grain dropped. To increase the supply of flour, barley was mixed with wheat. This hybrid flour produced bread that was dark grey in colour hence the name black bread.

The time of the black bread! Did you ever hear tell of that? Everything was rationed, the butter, the tea, and sugar was rationed. Two ounces of butter a head and one ounce of tea a head, and the black bread was terrible.

Peggy Reid

It would be a white Christmas in the bread shops for the brown loaf of the Emergency would disappear and be replaced by bread bearing a close colour kinship with the pre-war product. The new loaf would contain a 65 per cent wheat extraction compared with 75 per cent in peace time.

Irish Independent 11th November 1943.

From the beginning of the Emergency, ration books were issued by the Department of Supplies mainly for tea, sugar, butter, soap, clothes and footwear. Ration books became the one guaranteed way of securing food, as long as the items were available and regulations relating to their use and misuse were legion and covered all possible eventualities.

SPECIAL RATION BOOKS, FOOD RATION CARDS.
Persons coming to reside in the State, including temporary visitors, are not given General Ration Books unless they intend to remain here at least six months. Such persons can, however, obtain Food Ration Cards, covering one week's ration of tea, sugar and butter, if they intend to stay for more than five days.

Department of Supplies, 'Handbook issued for the Guidance of Shopkeepers' 1st July 1943.

Then in 1939 and from that year until it finished, we had to do with a ration. You had coupons for your butter; and coupons for your tea; and coupons for sugar; coupons for clothes.

Kitty Hughes

Along with rationing the Department of Supplies introduced price controls and quotas but naturally a black-market came into existence. The main source of black-market goods was Northern Ireland.

They used to smuggle, my father and other old people, do you know at that time you were allowed completely everything in Northern Ireland where there wasn't any ration?

Charlie Cawley, who is a Traveller.

Pure white bread was an impossibility unless you used someone who travelled North. They'd get the white flour and come home and make the bread, or they could buy white bread made in the North, you had to smuggle it down.

Patsy Magill

Throughout the Emergency the black-market flourished, providing not only goods to supplement the rations of those who could afford them but also healthy profits for those who ran the illicit trade. The tea ration varied between two ounces to half an ounce and could only be legally bought from recognised outlets and like flour was often adulterated to make it go further. There were various unrationed tea substitutes such as shell cocoa, made from the shells of cocoa beans, but these were as popular as the black bread. However tea was available on the black-market at the cost of £1 per pound of tea! This tea usually contained some additive such as hawthorn leaves or it was tea that had already been used and subsequently dried and then sold again as fresh tea. Fruit and vegetables were not rationed, but their availability was limited to what could be grown in Ireland. As well as relying on farm grown produce many people turned their gardens over to growing vegetables so as to supplement their diet. In the same way that tea and sugar were rationed, so were clothes and footwear. Without the necessary coupons new clothing simply could not be bought and this meant that not only did people re-cycle clothing by mending and altering them, but they also relied on jumble sales. And to guarantee that they had new clothes for important occasions like weddings or First Communions people would start using their coupons and paying for them months before they were needed.

There used to be jumble sales in them days, but you used to do the best you could. First Communion and that, we always got our clothes in the Warehouse. You'd start paying them off for months before they had it.

Kitty Hayes

Naturally, fuels such as coal, electricity, gas and petrol were also rationed. The electricity and gas companies regulated the supply of their commodities, only making them available at times of peak use.

Electricity became rationed very much then around 1942, we were very rationed in our digs. Well the gas; you'd get the gas for so long, maybe an hour in the middle of the day; an hour in the morning and an hour in the evening.

Kitty Hayes

Owing to a serious breakdown in the gas-making plant of the Alliance and Dublin Consumers Gas Co., the hours of supply in Dublin were being curtailed until repairs were carried out. The early morning hours of 5.30 to 8 a.m. were unaffected, but the day hours would be 11.30 a.m. to 1 p.m. instead of 1.30; and the evening hours would be 6 to 7 p.m., instead of 8 p.m.

Irish Independent 24th November 1943

Whilst the electricity supply was simply turned off at source, which effectively prohibited its use outside of the prescribed times, it was possible to use the gas supply after it had been turned off as a residue of gas was left in the pipes. However, it was illegal to use this, as there was a danger that without continuous pressure airlocks would form in the pipes thereby blocking them and causing problems for all users. 'Glimmermen' were employed to ensure that gas was not being illicitly used and if caught the supply would be disconnected.

Well there would be some gas left in the pipes and you could use that. But it was very dangerous, because it might light back into the pipe. So there was what they called the Glimmerman. That was a glimmer, 'twould only be a glimmer, but it would boil milk or something for you. But the Glimmerman used to go around and he'd knock at doors and several of my pals wouldn't let him in because even if you turned it off the gas (ring) would still be hot. But when we were in Howth, it never troubled us because with the height of Howth there was a good glimmer and so you didn't open the door anyway until it was well off.

Kitty Hayes

Petrol rationing was introduced almost immediately following the declaration of the state of Emergency in 1939. Despite stringent control of existing fuel stocks it was inevitable that eventually private motoring would be impossible as the war dragged on and what supplies existed would be given over to priority needs. By 1942 the vast majority of private cars were off the roads and would remain so until the end of the war. A lot of the garages that had started life as bicycle shops now had to fall back on that trade.

During the war years not many would have petrol, it was hard to get, it was really hard but you had the odd few who could do it.

Jack Buckley

We were greatly restricted and there was a time that we didn't have cars on the road at all. And the petrol rationing was really draconian and they, I must say that the government did, they were forced by circumstances to really enforce the law with regards to all this.

Wilf Fitzsimmons, former president of the Royal Irish Automobile Club.

Very quickly people came to rely on bicycles and horse-power. Throughout the war the horse enjoyed a revival, working once more in rural and urban areas. And for those who worked in trades and crafts associated with the horse; such as blacksmiths and harness makers, the war years were a brief respite from the decline of their respective crafts which the automobile's introduction into Ireland had started.

There wasn't a lot of alternatives. There was bicycles and of course a lot of people, they went back to horse transport. My own firm, we were book publishers, we used to deliver to the schools with a couple of horse-drawn vehicles. There was petrol for very, very vital things, but there certainly wasn't petrol for anything that was frivolous.

Wilf Fitzsimmons

Oh the cars, well they were in use when I was at school, but then during the war on account of petrol rationing the only cars you'd see were doctors and I think priests had them for a sick call. The deliveries were done mainly on horses; reverted to horse again. It was all cycling. Did you ever see pictures of O'Connell street? We were all cycling.

Kitty Hayes

An alternative existed for the enterprising motorist and that was to convert their car to run on gas. There were two methods of doing this. The first was to attach a large gas-bag to the roof of your car which would be filled up at the local gas company. On cars like a Ford Prefect this would allow you roughly 50 miles motoring. The alternative to this was the charcoal burning gas producer;

> *Then of course there was the gas producers which you hung either on the back or on the front that burnt charcoal or anthracite. Most of them worked, but some of them were a bit more sophisticated and they did work well. The great problem was getting charcoal which was free of certain impurities which gave you a great clinker so you'd be going along and everything would stop.*

Wilf Fitzsimmons

> *This vet opposite us, he had some kind of a gas yoke on the back of his car alright, because he had to go out at night and all, but there was very few cars on the roads.*

Bernadette Marks

The end of the war brought some relief to Ireland's petrol rationing, but it was not until 1951 that petrol became freely available again. By the end of the Emergency, Ireland had an economy which was stagnant having endured five years shortages of imported raw materials and manufactured goods. It is ironic, given Ireland's neutrality, that the worst year Ireland suffered in relation to the Emergency was in fact 1947 when a combination of bad weather, fuel and food shortages combined to bring about real hardship.

> *It wasn't till after I was married did it become very bad. The worst year would have been about 1947, when the war was over and that was the year, people called it the Famine Black '47, but that was the year we had snow from January till March 1947. And the turf was at its worst, because the year before had been bad and they were selling turf wringing wet because it was sold by weight. It was all turf, coal was finished. But 1947, even though the war was over, was the worst year I think in rationing and all, because a lot of the Merchant Navy had been killed in the war and they were the real heroes of the war from our point of view. Everything was scarce; like tea, sugar was rationed.*

Kitty Hayes

THE POST OFFICE

One of the greatest thrills of the week for many people was to get letters back from America and England. It was a matter of getting their letter to find out how the person was.

Jack Buckley

The postal system was the most important and widely used form of communication throughout this period. Telephone ownership was still very low, in fact by the end of 1959 just over 5% of the population owned a telephone. The telephones that were owned tended to be on commercial premises, and although the first public telephone had been introduced in 1925, even into the 1950's they were still a rarity in some parts of rural Ireland.

The telephone wasn't so widely available 'til the last twenty years. Business, 'twas business operations mainly, but for private houses the telephone wasn't considered all that big a necessity. You didn't have any other means of communication (apart from the post), then a stamp only cost a penny or tuppence.

Jack Buckley

Maureen Weir was the post mistress of the sub-post office on the Main Street in Swords for sixteen years. Local post offices then not only carried out many of the duties we would normally associate with them, but they also ran what in effect was a local sorting office and telegram office. Prior to working in Swords she had been an assistant in a post office and had moved to Swords on securing employment there.

Well at that time I was in County Meath, working in a post office there and I was at it a good few years. I was thirty sevenish I'd say when I came here and it was time for me to get an office of my own 'cause all I was getting was ten bob a week or twelve and six or something like that, as assistant at that time. So I applied for the post office, and because I had experience I got it. I have been a post office worker all my life, sub-post office. Now that isn't anything like the Head Office, you do exams to get into Head Office. You do an interview all right and if you'd already had experience in sub-post offices well that helps you get a position. So anyway I was appointed in Swords.

Maureen Weir

Running a sub-post office entailed a large amount of responsibility and necessitated working long hours.

When I took it over I was responsible for four postmen and I had to have an assistant as well. The mail came in at a quarter to seven in the morning, so you had to do the mail work and be with the postmen; sort the letters, do the registers and get the postmen on their rounds. So it would be hell for leather between a quarter to seven and nine o'clock to get all that work cleared out.

Maureen Weir

Although the post office closed at six, this did not mean that Maureen's working day was over as there was always more work to do and this included dealing with telegrams.

I had to do the counter work from nine until six, but it went on till eight really. You signed a document which meant that at any time work would come up that you'd have to do until eight o'clock at night. On top of all that then, we had to deliver telegrams and we used to get telegrams from all arts and parts with no appointed messenger, you had to do it yourself or go out on the streets and beg; if I meet you or you or someone and say 'Would you ever be going such a direction, would you mind bringing a telegram?'

Maureen Weir

Telegrams had to be delivered regardless of the day or the hour and this could mean that the post mistress had to work after the office had closed. They were also expected to be open on Sundays and even at Christmas.

I often had to go in and I'd close the door at six o'clock and get a cup of tea, put my coat and hat on me, and go out the road two or three miles with the telegram after being on my feet all day from half six in the morning. Sunday morning was nine to half ten you had to take the telegrams, that's if there was any, for the area. And it was the same at Christmas, Christmas day, and Stephen's day. Oh Lord 'twas fierce, at the end of the day we'd two or three telegrams sittin' down on the desk and they'd have to be delivered. Well, that's the life I had for the best part of sixteen years.

Maureen Weir

Work would finally end with the day's accounts being checked and balanced. Sub-post offices had their books randomly audited and it was important that the accounts were kept in good order.

The efficiency, 100% was demanded from you and you never knew when what we called checkers or inspectors would come out from Head Office and start checking your accounts. I remember one morning at half past eight and the postmen were just going out and I was going to go in and make a cup of tea and I looked out the window and I see's this inspector standing outside. He would check the accounts and of course, if you were short you'd have to state what happened. A few times they came anyway and I was dead on, and I was delighted.

Maureen Weir

Just as Maureen had been a postal assistant in County Meath, when she was working in Swords she had to employ girls to work with her but, given the conditions of employment, it was often difficult to attract girls to take up positions in the sub-post office.

It was hard to get girls. It was hard to get assistants then 'cause I wasn't getting the money myself, I'd to pay the girl out of my own wages. I still think what was allotted to us was terrible. It was hard to get assistants then and I was always as good as I could be to them and there'd always be plenty of tea going and the radio on in the kitchen.

Maureen Weir

The frustrations the job engendered meant that girls would often leave if other jobs became available or failing that, emigrate to seek work.

Well I had one girl that worked for me, she was very good, great at figures. It was a big loss to me when I lost her. But she was going to go, she said to me 'Look, I know all that's to be known about the post office, and I'll never get any further,' and she said 'I'm going to go to America.' And she did and she did very well in it.

Maureen Weir

Regardless of the responsibility, the amount of work involved and the requirement to pay their assistants from their own money, the wages paid to those running the sub-post offices were very low and benefits such as pensions or holiday pay only became available at a later stage.

I won't tell you what the few shillings I was getting for doing that, you wouldn't wash the delph for it now, what I was getting a week. I didn't take a holiday, it was three or four or five years before I could afford to take a holiday then. I think in the beginning we didn't, but then towards the end, we were getting some kind of an allowance towards it, you know. You'd have to get someone else to run it, and give them money to do it out of your own money. Conditions were awful in the sub-post office. No, no pension schemes. Now when I gave up, I think I got a £100. There was no money in it, you didn't get a pension out of it because it wasn't Civil Service.

Maureen Weir

The major outside factor which brought change to sub-post offices was the growth of rural towns like Swords. As Swords grew the demands on the post grew. Larger premises were needed for sorting the mail and providing a more efficient service to the community.

When I came to Swords there was only that Seatown Villas and there was what they called the Twelve Apostles, twelve cottages out on the Rathbeale Road. And that was all that was in it. After that then, Glassmore extended and Rathbeale, they were the first two of new housing schemes and then after that River Valley. When the place was getting bigger they wanted me to buy another place, provide them with a place to sort the letters and all that kind of thing. Swords was getting bigger all the time.

Maureen Weir

Eventually the nature of the work done in sub-post offices changed and from the 1940's onwards the Post Office revised the postal service in rural areas to make it more effective. As aspects of the work like sorting mail and the telegraph service become more centralised, sub-post offices increasingly became part of other shops.

When you look at them now, nine until half past five, they've no telegrams, they've no postmen. They're only dealing with the people coming in to get stamps and postal orders and money orders and that kind of thing. You see that's why sub-post offices are mainly in shops where people have a business already and they're not depending on that.

Maureen Weir

THE HOSIERY FACTORY AND THE DRESSMAKER

Smyth and Company Hosiery is the largest employer in the town and employs between the indoor and outdoor staff, roughly 600. The majority of these are girls and the chief articles of manufacture are ladies, gents and children's hose, and ladies and gents underwear.

Drogheda Independent 1937

The hosiery factory of Smyth's of Balbriggan had come into existence in 1780 and was to produce a variety of hosiery for the next two hundred years. Its origins lay in a cottage industry reputed to have been carried out in the Balrothery area since before 1740, which made and supplied hosiery for Balbriggan and Dublin. Throughout the following century and a half the factory, and the reputation of its products went from strength to strength. The name Balbriggan, which was inscribed on their products, became the hallmark of high quality hosiery to such an extent that it became a generic term within the hosiery industry.

It (Balbriggan) was so successful with the hosiery industry that other people were copying the name Balbriggan and at one stage a company in England was selling their product as genuine English Balbriggans.

Joe Curtis, whose father worked in the hosiery factory.

The Economic War with Britain placed Smyth & Co. in a very strong position. Tariffs on imported British hosiery made their prices prohibitive for the Irish market and the factory operated at full capacity to meet orders for the home market.

They were working 24 hours a day, divided into 3 sections. So they were really extremely busy at that time.

Joe Curtis

The factory was a major source of employment at this time in Balbriggan and although the production of hosiery was highly mechanised, the work was still very labour intensive. Within the factory there existed a hierarchy with hosiers occupying the top position on the factory floor and their importance was reflected in their wage.

I would say of permanent employees, I would say the maximum number they would have had would have been about somewhere around 350 or 400. Permanent employees. The hosier was the highest paid of all the people other than the management. And the hosier's job would have been a very skilled job, it would have been the cream job to have had. In the 1950's a hosier would have been earning about twice what a carpenter or a fitter would have been. They would have been earning £15 at that time and a fitter would have been earning about £8.16s. You had to serve your apprenticeship to your father, that was how it was done all the time.

Joe Curtis

That was the job, the hosier. We're talking about fully fashioned hosiery. The kingpins, they were kings. Most of them would be on two shifts when there would be orders in.

Bill Hamilton who worked in the hosiery factory.

The complexity involved in making even the ordinary stockings illustrates how many people were involved in production. Initially the basic web, the material that made the stocking, was fashioned on a loom. The seamless type were joined by machines or if seemed stockings, by hand.

You take the ordinary stockings then. It was unbelievable, the work that went into that. It had to be knitted, it had to be welted, it had to be toed, turned off we used to call it. Seamed, if there was a seam wanted. Then it had to be mended. It had to go to a girl who'd examine it all over for any flaws. Every stocking had to be examined by the menders. Then it would have to go to the assembly room, sorted into different sizes, cottons, silks, lyle.

Bill Hamilton

Once they had been checked for any flaws such as dropped stitches the stocks had to be washed and dyed.

The goods went into the wash house and they had to be washed, thoroughly washed and the dyer would come along and he had to compound the dye for whatever number of dozens that was in the lot. Then they would be dyed. There'd be maybe one or two stockings taken out.

Bill Hamilton

They had shade cards there to see if it was right and if it was brighter they'd have to bring it back and darken it a little.

Nellie Hamilton, who worked in the hosiery factory.

Now if the dye was not right, they had to be washed again. Now it had to be dried, put in a big tumble dryer. Now it was brought back into the girls. That was the assembly.

Bill Hamilton

Once dyed, they were ready to be trimmed, sized and finally dispatched.

Now they were brought into the girls in the trim shop. And they started immediately trimming them and sorting out the sizes. The trimmer came along and he trimmed them all up. Now they were all put on flat boards, all carried into the folding room. Now, they were put into pairs, the folder folded them and then from the folders to dispatch.

Bill Hamilton

As well as the men and women who were employed in the factory, women in Balbriggan took work in. Their work varied from minor repairs to finishing work and of course the embroidery of 'Balbriggan' across the stocking tops.

They also had a lot of seasonal workers and they had a good deal of 'outwork' for want of a better word. I suppose it was work that was sent around to people's houses and what they would do was they would have a van, they would deliver round the work and collect it a couple of days later. They would mostly do mendings of slightly defective, if there was one stitch dropped. They would also do things like turning over the top of the stocking, it's kind of the elasticated thing at the top of the stocking. We tend to forget people take it almost for granted now, there was no such things as tights; that was pre-tights.

Joe Curtis

The outside workers, my mother did that. They used to do threading and mending. A lot of people got work. It was nice to see them writing 'Balbriggan' in red across the top of the stocking, embroidery.

Nellie Hamilton

Stockings became damaged during production if any fluff from the yarn got into the looms as they were working. This meant that there was no ventilation in the machine shops because of the problem draughts would cause.

It was very hot, the machines you see. We had all types of machinery then making ankle socks, men's socks, ladies ankle socks. If you did open (a window) there'd be a draught, the fluff would get on the machine, get on the yarn.

Bill Hamilton

At the height of production the machines were kept running the whole time, not only to meet the demands of the Irish market but because the men operating them were paid for the output of the machine they were operating.

There was no such thing as stopping machinery. When you were on the day work you got your tea sent over to you. When you were on the 4 to 12 you got your lunch sent to you. You didn't stop machinery, you could if you liked, but you were losing money. You got paid so much per dozen.

Bill Hamilton

This practice also made for high wages for machine operators.

I remember one time, 1946, '47, we got a big order from Sweden and they wanted kiddies socks. And that order lasted three of us, that was Tom Curtis, Doug Archbold and myself 16, 18 weeks. We had the highest wages. My average wages at that particular time was £60 a week. Unheard of! That was a terrific order.

Bill Hamilton

Whilst this system of payment had its advantages, in times of low demand or shortages of raw materials, it meant that the loom would lie idle and the workers would go unpaid.

During the war things were very bad, you couldn't get material. The gang would be saying then, 'Is the yarn in yet?' 'No, its at Greenore.' Greenore down at Omeath in the North of Ireland. The yarn used to come in there. Then up by train into Balbriggan, the station was right beside the factory. The war years, you worked as you got the raw material.

Bill Hamilton

At times like these, factory workers would have to find temporary work.

To try and bring up your wages when your wages were bad we used to go up at 5 o'clock in the morning to pick the winkles. There was more money made with the winkles than there was with Smyth's at that time. A lad from Dundalk used to collect them. We started then to cut out the middle man and sell them to Billingsgate, London.

Nellie Hamilton

From the thirties onwards Smyth and Co. had started to diversify their line of products to include mass produced hosiery, a move away from their more expensive, exclusive lines. This was to compete with the rise in cheap imports. Initially this policy worked well, but following the end of World War II and the resumption of international trade they found it hard to hold their place in the market. Increasingly factory workers had to rely on other sources of income, normally taking agricultural work.

I can remember my father, when the hosiery industry started to get that there wasn't full employment in it, I suppose they were the bad old times in the mid 50's and Smyths was beginning to experience difficult times and one of the things was the threshing mills were still very much on the go and picking potatoes, that was still done by hand, my father would do that kind of work.

Joe Curtis

Naturally this type of work was very hard on the hands and factory workers had to ensure that their nails and hands did not become rough and calloused.

When he'd come home in the evening from working at a mill or whatever, he used to get cream and rub the cream into his hands and we used to think he was very sissy but we didn't understand that when he got the shout to go back to the factory the men's hands had to be kept immaculate. They had to be kept perfect because every little snag that you put on a stocking cost you money. You got less money for it. They were counted as seconds. My father would be at this and I used to see Mammy and she used have a little piece of fine emery paper, 400 or 600, emery paper and she would smooth, you know the quicks of his nails, and she would do his nails for him. The importance of it was, if he got back into full-time employment his hands had to be in perfect condition. He couldn't have welts, none of the hosiers could.

Joe Curtis

Smyth's Hosiery Factory and the way it was developing in this period illustrated the way the clothing industry in general was changing. Increasingly, clothes were becoming mass produced, replacing the traditional trades of tailors and dressmakers. Nevertheless, these trades were still being practised throughout Fingal. People relied upon tailors and dressmakers to make them new clothes, and to repair and adapt older garments. To secure an apprenticeship with a dressmaker was very desirable as the job offered both security and the potential to make a good living. Mary Lowndes, originally from Rush and now living in Swords, was still attending school when her mother secured for her a place with a dressmaker.

My mother had asked her would she take me, that I liked sewing. Children were queuing up to get their trade with her. I was going to do my Inter in June and I left school in March because if I missed that apprenticeship I wouldn't get another go.

Mary Lowndes

Dressmaking businesses were traditionally small concerns, businesses run by one or two women.

There was really only herself and there would be two apprentices, it was only a small business. It was only twelve and sixpence to have a dress made then. That was the dearest to have your dress made. A suit was £2 and 10 shillings.

Mary Lowndes

Girls were taken on for three years to learn the trade of dressmaking. Unlike apprenticeships, governed by guilds and trade bodies, the arrangement was a lot more informal.

I served my time with a girl from Rush, I served three years with her, and I served my time for nothing, you paid nothing and you got your trade. They called it serving your time then, not getting your apprenticeship. And I served my time there for three years and she paid me nothing and my mother didn't pay her anything.

Mary Lowndes

72

Whilst she was learning to become a dressmaker Mary's parents continued to support her until she went into business for herself.

You see we had a very simple life, it was only a shilling to go to the pictures and we used to go to a one and six penny hop in Rush on a Wednesday night and then go to a dance on a Sunday night, my father would give me the half-crown on a Sunday night and my mother would give me the one and six on a Wednesday night. As for clothes, when my mother had to buy them, she bought the material and I made them.

Mary Lowndes

The process of learning to become a dressmaker was slow. Over the three years, the apprentice was gradually introduced to the different skills and tasks she would need as a dressmaker. Jobs such as tacking, lightly sewing two pieces of cloth together, where taught through repetition.

You started at nine in the morning and you finished at six in the evening and you had a half day on a Monday. Your role in the first year was tacking, she would cut out all this gear and hand it to you to tack, and you'd tack and tack and tack. The second year you might get a go on the machine and on the third you'd be allowed to put a garment together. You'd have to set in the sleeve, and you could put it in three, or four, or five times and take it out and put it all back in again. All depending on what flair you had for the dressmaking. You just sat for the whole of the first year tacking but she didn't allow you to cut out or anything, you had to buy material yourself and make something yourself, but she had patterns that she used like for herself. Then you were allowed to cut them out when you were going, that was a big deal.

Mary Lowndes

Once the three years were up, the girl was able to go into business for herself. Unlike many of the other areas in which women were employed at this time, such as in domestic service or in the Civil Service, marriage did not mean an end to her working career because as she was self-employed the dressmaker was able to continue working. Interestingly, married women could also carry on work in the hosiery factory.

I worked for abut six months after I got married, about six months. You had to ask permission could you come back to work. Then I left, I hadn't the time, not with all the children in this house.

Nellie Hamilton

I had my three years done and I just left then. So when I finished my time, my father built me a sewing room at the side of the house and I worked there until I got married and even when I got married I kept up my little business. And then, you got to hear I was sewing and somebody else got to hear I was sewing and I had my customers. I had a lot of customers who came from Swords to me. And people that went to the woman I served my time with, they came over to me because they would be friends in fact.

Mary Lowndes

As with so many trades in this period, dressmakers worked long hours. After their work in the day, they would have customers coming to them in the evening.

You'd be finished at six o'clock, sewing, and then you'd have your clients coming to you, they'd come in the evening time to get fitted. And you fitted them and then you had to take that asunder the next day, re-cut it, put it back together again, re-fit them again another evening and then finish the garment. It could be eight or nine o'clock before you'd be finished.

Mary Lowndes

The money a dressmaker earned varied from week to week, and depended on the level of work she had during any one period.

One week you might earn £20, the next you might make £40. It all depended on what you got through, you'd no set wage, but there was men working for £6 and £7 a week. There was no slack time, because there was always children's summer clothes, and then there was the childen's winter clothes.

Mary Lowndes

Mary Lowndes' clientele were drawn predominantly from local women and children.

You see I wasn't in the tailoring end of it. That's a completely different trade all together, tailoring. Well they were doing men, you know we only made for women, that's all I did. I never worked in a factory or, in with a group of people, just on my own. That's all, just women's clothes. We didn't do men's clothes, no we didn't do men, just women and children.

Mary Lowndes

The type of work that dressmakers did varied from making up new garments to altering and repairing old clothes

Your mother would come with her coat and it'd be ripped and she'd get a coat made out of it for you or she'd bring a coat belonging to herself and she'd get it turned and re-lined. This out here and this in here and it would look new again and it would be re-lined. We used to make skirts, uniforms for schools, the gym slips, they were for the Holy Faith in Skerries. I made the soutane and the surplice for a priest, he was ordained in Rush and I also made altar boys' clothes. And I made a nun's clothes, her habit and her head gear. I did bride dresses and brides-maids' dresses, scores of them. And I did loads of dresses for girls in Swords that got married. And I did my own, and I did my daughter's up a couple of years ago.

Mary Lowndes

Although dressmakers had sewing machines and irons, their application was very basic and a lot of work still had to be done by hand.

It was just ordinary household machines. Buttonholes had to be done by hand and the buttons had to be put in by hand. Now we have machines that do button holes and sew in buttons and do embroidery and everything on them. In those days they were just ordinary household machines and you had to hand sew the buttonholes, a skill in itself, to make it all even and make it all look nice. There was another thing in dressmaking, you had to finish a thing very well. Pressing it, there was no steam irons then either, there were big heavy irons and you had a piece of maybe white hanky or white cotton and it was wet and it steamed everything, every seam was steamed and pressed, everything was well finished.

Mary Lowndes

Clothes were made to a very high standard as the reliance on hand work as opposed to machining meant that a lot of care was taken finishing the garments.

When we used to put darts into dresses now, when the garment was finished, it had to be turned inside out and everyone of those had to have, they were all tied, a knot tied on them. Then trimmed, and the seams were all trimmed and your padding was all put in properly, stitched in. Not a stitch here and a stitch there, it was stitched all around then. There was canvas all put in the front of the jackets that made them good and stiff. Then they sat properly, there's nothing now, just nothing at all. It's all mass production now.

Mary Lowndes

Dressmaking and the hosiery factory both went into decline for the same reason, they were unable to compete with mass produced cheaper clothing. In a reversal of the situation in the 40's and 50's, handmade clothes became the preserve of the wealthy.

And the material was brilliant then, you could buy gabardine, pure wool materials for about £2 a yard and three yards made you a jacket and skirt. The material was brilliant, it would last you for a life time. Poor people got their clothes made, not the rich people. The rich people would go into Sloweys or Arnotts or some of those places. Sloweys it was a store, you'd pay a fortune for things in it. I'd love it if there was more dressmakers around and if it was a thing that was done, I think its a beautiful craft and the clothes were of much better quality.

Mary Lowndes

By the end of the fifties the factory in Balbriggan was starting to experience the problems which would bring about its closure and the next decade saw the introduction of a phase-out plan, and eventually its closure in 1980.

It was the job. Balbriggan at that particular time used to be the capital of Fingal. The money was in Balbriggan because of the factory. Now there's nothing, absolutely nothing.

Bill Hamilton

CONCLUSION

Things change, they're never the same. This area has probably trebled in population. Being honest I've never seen the country looking so beautiful and good. I've never seen crops so good, I've never seen the wildlife so good.

Noel McAllister

Between 1936 and 1959 working life in Fingal changed in a fundamental manner under the pressures of progress and modernisation. Traditional farm life and the way the work was done on farms changed irrevocably due to innovations such as the tractor and piped water. And whilst they alleviated many of the hardships associated with rural work, they also brought with them pressure for farms to be increasingly worked as businesses. These changes radiated out from the farms in Fingal to the wider rural community leaving no area of work untouched. The changes to working life were often slow and they did bring many benefits with them but nevertheless they gradually eroded a working life which is now consigned to memory.

BIBLIOGRAPHY

T. Brown — Ireland, A Social and Cultural History 1922-1979.
Fontana 1982

L. Byrne — The History of Aviation in Ireland.
Blackwater Press 1980

E. Estyn Evans — Irish Heritage: The Landscape, The People and Their Work **Dundalk 1943**

Evans, Routledge & Keegan Paul (eds.) — Irish Folk Ways **London 1957**

M. Hearn — Below Stairs, Domestic ·Service Remembered in Dublin and Beyond 1880-1922.
Lilliput Press 1993

Kennedy, Giblin & McHugh — The Economic Development of Ireland in the 20th Century. **Routledge 1988**

F.S.L. Lyons — Ireland Since the Famine. **Fontana 1982**

O'Brien & Dalton (eds.) — Crafts of Ireland. **Dublin 1979**

S. O'Broin — The Book of Finglas. **Kincora Press 1980**

T. O'Neill — Life and Tradition in Rural Ireland. **Dent 1977**

G. O Riain — Traveller Ways Traveller Words.
Pavee Point Publications

S. O Suilleabhain — A Handbook of Irish Folklore.
**The Educational Company of Ireland Ltd.
for The Folklore of Ireland Society 1942.**

M. Ludd & C. Murphy — Women Surviving. **Poolbeg 1990**

J. Meenan — The Irish Economy Since 1922. **Liverpool 1970**

C.H. Murray   The Civil Service Observed.
                                 The Institute of Public Administration 1990

K. Nowlan (ed)   Travel and Transport in Ireland.
                                 Gill & Macmillan 1973

Nowlan & Williams (eds.)   Ireland in the War Years and After 1939-1951.

H. Oram   Dublin Airport The History.
                                 Criterion Press 1990

M.J. Shiel   The Quiet Revolution: The Electrification of
                                 Rural Ireland.   **O'Brien Press 1984**

Telecom Eireann   Recalling - The Telephone in Ireland, How It All
                                 Began.   **Telecom Eireann 1991**

W.C.C. & C.   Ten Dublin Women   Women's Commemorative
                                 Celebration Committee.   **Dublin 1991**

PERIODICALS

Drogheda Independent

Fingal Fingerpost

History Ireland   Vol. 1. No. 2 Summer 1993 'Dancing Depravity
                                 and all that Jazz' by Jim Smyth, pp. 51-54

Irish Farmers Journal

Irish Independent

Irish Times